Praise for
The Board of Directors: for
a Private Enterprise

"Your book is an amazing piece of work. You are setting a new standard for a real-world advisory guide on boards of directors: why have one, and how to recruit for, form, run, and get value from a board. You have done yourself proud. This book reflects your vast body of experience coupled with superb writing talent, resulting in a guidebook that will be helpful to management and board members of not only the smaller and privately owned company but of established public companies as well."
- James Kristie, Former Editor & Associate Publisher, Directors & Boards Magazine

"This book should be required reading for all entrepreneurs and VC firms. I particularly enjoyed the war stories on the Director Firings!"
- Don Daseke, President & CEO, Daseke Inc.

"I have finally had a chance to peruse the new book that you sent. This is excellent! There is such a huge gap in understanding on the part of private companies, startups, etc., as to 'all things governance'. Your book does a great job filling in this huge gap. I wish you the best of success with the book."
-Henry D. Wolfe, Chairman De La Vega Occidental & Oriental Holdings L.L.C.

"Full of practical examples of how boards can work and improve themselves. This is really, really good stuff."
- John Adler, Former Partner, Silver Creek Ventures

"What a treat! It brought me back to some good and bad times. A must-read for any businessperson looking to run organizations. Thank you."
- **Steve Sandquist, President, Sandquist Consulting**

"This book is of genuine value. I do believe in the 'independent' board for private companies, but just as Mr. Kristie, judge that there is a dearth of good advice on how to recruit, develop, and lead such boards. Yours will be a very worthwhile contribution to the field, and a book that I will recommend to the many in the audience that shudder at the task of building that first board.

Some specifics: Superb calling out of the need for documentation. I see frequent instances where this aspect is either overlooked or simply seen as too much effort. It is the first indication of the desire to be seen as 'growing up' or, if you will, professionalizing the organization.

You are spot on with your observation regarding recruitment that 'you can often learn more about them from the questions they ask you than the ones you ask them'.

Your treatment of comparing the fiduciary board versus the advisory board is the best explanation I have ever seen. And it is a question on the minds of many private companies that I have visited.

Kudos on this wonderful contribution to the family business segment!"
- **Jim Ethier, Former Chairman, Bush Brothers & Company**

The Board of Directors
for a Private Enterprise

*A comprehensive inside look
at creating and managing the boards
of private companies of all types*

DENNIS J. CAGAN

authorHOUSE®

AuthorHouse™
1663 Liberty Drive
Bloomington, IN 47403
www.authorhouse.com
Phone: 1 (800) 839-8640

Published by AuthorHouse 03/21/2017

ISBN: 978-1-5246-6015-4 (sc)
ISBN: 978-1-5246-6016-1 (e)

Print information available on the last page.

Any people depicted in stock imagery provided by Thinkstock are models,
and such images are being used for illustrative purposes only.
Certain stock imagery © Thinkstock.

This book is printed on acid-free paper.

This book is dedicated to the hundreds of board directors, executives, and managers that I have had the honor to serve with on fiduciary boards of directors over the last five decades. Collectively these men and women have demonstrated the best in American corporate governance, and unfortunately, at times, some not-so-good behavior. However, I have studied and tried to learn from it (them) all.

This entire body of knowledge and experience has taught me many hard-learned and sometimes expensive lessons, and allowed me to better understand the demands of good corporate governance. Thank you one and all. I am honored to have served with each of you.

There are three individuals without whom I might not have found the perseverance to complete this book. Thank you especially to Jim Kristie, Max Toy and Bill Bergeron for their counsel, inspiration and help.

Special thanks go to my wife Angelia, who is much smarter than I, and still teaching me the principals of good governance – especially at the family level; and my daughter Sydney who at age eleven inspired me when she self-published a book of her own poetry, and again at thirteen published a children's book.

God bless you all.

About the Author

Dennis Cagan is a high-technology industry veteran, seasoned director, and entrepreneur, having founded over a dozen different companies. He co-founded his first software company in 1968.

In 1976 Mr. Cagan founded his fifth company, and in 1980 it was ranked #32 on the first *Inc. Magazine* 'Inc. 100.' His first public board seat was when the company was listed on NASDAQ in February 1981. Since 1968 Mr. Cagan has served on sixty corporate fiduciary boards, both public and private, predominantly early and mid-stage technology companies.

Mr. Cagan is widely known for his usual dress, a Hawaiian shirt.

Mr. Cagan is a seasoned founder, CEO/Chairman, and has been a C-level executive (both public and private companies), venture capitalist, private investor, consultant and professional board member for almost five decades. In 1979, Dennis was the Keynote Speaker at the first COMDEX Show in Las Vegas. In 2011, he was inducted into the IT Hall of Fame - Channel Wing, administered by CompTIA. In 2013, the Dallas Business Journal and NACD selected him as one of twelve Outstanding Directors in North Texas. Mr. Cagan now consults on forming boards, augments management teams as a

Shadow CEO™, and periodically serves in an interim CEO capacity. He resides in the Dallas area with his wife Angelia and their youngest daughter.

He can be contacted at dennis@caganco.com.

Table of Contents

Why did I write this book, and for whom did I write it?

Overview

This book is written for anyone who works for, manages or owns a private company. It is also directed toward those who aspire to be on a board of directors – whether a privately owned company, public enterprise, or non-profit organization.

When you have completed reading this book, you will have a comprehensive real-life understanding of what a board of directors does, how it does it; how to start, build, and run a board, and most importantly, an insight into the incredible value that a good board can deliver to any organization. In addition, also included is a wealth of detailed information about all aspects of corporate governance, and its practical application. All of this is accompanied by personal anecdotes. While I focus on best-of-class private company governance, the material is directly applicable to public companies and non-profits.

Backstory

I was standing at my kitchen countertop one evening, doing the dinner dishes and thinking about the chapter of this book I was working on at the time. It's the one about compensation, which was by far the most difficult to write. I'd been stuck on the chapter for at least two days and I was starting to become frustrated. I knew what I wanted to say but getting it down on paper was defeating me. More than once the thought had occurred to me, *why did I ever decide to write this book; and for whom was I writing it?*

Since this was my thirteenth chapter, it was probably a little late to be thinking about this, however my thoughts took me down an interesting path.

I have started a number of companies. Some did moderately well. In 1981 I successfully took my fifth company public and sold it a year later. Another one which I founded in 1985 achieved $22MM in revenue in its very first year in business. Others were frankly mediocre. I had a touch, but I wouldn't call it exactly *golden*. For most of my career I was a salesman, and still remain one at heart. The one thing that stands out to me about my career is that I have done an unusually wide variety of things: I have started a number of companies, I've held a number of different positions, I've had the privilege of being CEO of several companies.

I started in the computer industry with IBM in 1967. In 1968, I co-founded my first software company – remote access computing application software. As a result, I've been in the information technology field now for five decades. I've been closely associated with companies providing software, hardware, IT systems and services, semiconductors, computer graphics, datacom, Internet, infrastructure, e-commerce, social media, manufacturing, distribution, workplace training, mobile applications, wireless, cyber security, data analytics, internet-of-things, software-as-a-service, and more.

After all of this I have come to the conclusion that there's one thing I know really well and that's how to be an effective board member, particularly of private, earlier stage and mid-cap companies.

The first board I sat on was my own company. I admit in all candor that I did not start off being a good board member; but I feel that over the years I have become an expert. I attribute this to two things.

The first is that over my career I've made just about every mistake a business leader could make. The second is over the years I have had the privilege of sitting on boards with hundreds of the most knowledgeable, experienced, successful, objective, visionary, sensible, congenial men and women ever to sit on a board and as you can imagine, there were also some that were none of the above. I have tried to learn from it all.

Over the years I had been encouraged by friends to write a book. However, I was never convinced about the best topic. I kept coming back to four factors:

1. I could only write a book if I felt I was uniquely qualified on the subject.
2. I could only write a book if I felt I had sufficient material to actually comprise a *book*, however much that might be.
3. I could only write a book if I felt that there was a reasonable audience for the work, and one that would benefit from my writing.
4. I only wanted to write a book if I felt that it would be a somewhat original contribution to its field.

A few months prior to starting the book I had just completed a nine-month interim CEO engagement. As I was preparing to go back to my full-time consulting activities, I was contemplating some of those deep things that one thinks about as they grow older. Looking back on my career, I tried to take an honest inventory of those things I was not good at, the things I was pretty good at, and perhaps some in which I really was an expert. There were several skills, positions or categories that I thought I might be legitimately judged 'good' at. However, for most of those, I knew others who I felt were far better than I.

Then it came to me...

Based on my board of directors experience – the variety, depth, number, and performance, I felt I had identified my strong suit. As I researched books on boards, most seemed to be about the boards of large well-known public companies, yet there are millions of private firms of all sizes and types. The subject of boards for these organizations could definitely use some literary coverage. When I narrowed the research down to private company boards and governance, I found that there were almost no books on the subject. As part of my research, I interviewed business leaders, colleagues, educators, and some editors of business publications. Almost everyone enthusiastically endorsed the need for such a book.

In this book, I have synthesized the body of knowledge that I have gained from sixty corporate for-profit boards to date, over the last five decades. The information, education and opinion that I provide here comes directly from having lived through making just about every mistake possible during my career, and learning from those experiences.

What better basis is there for one's education and growth? Much of this stuff is not taught in classrooms or seminars. I have been told, over many years, that my being able to share a relevant experience, at the appropriate time, including anecdotes about failures as well as successes, has been an invaluable contribution to hundreds and hundreds of entrepreneurs, CEOs, business owners and leaders. I sincerely hope that you find similar value.

Chapter 1

Why Form a Board of Directors... and Why Not?

As the owner, CEO, or substantial shareholder of a private company, when did the thought of a board of directors first come to you? How did the idea come up? Did you read an article in a business publication? Did it come up in a conversation with company colleagues, or the owner of another company? Were you looking at another company, perhaps a competitor, and noticed that they had a board? Or, did it simply occur to you one day that perhaps you could be more successful if you assembled a small group of experts to advise you at the highest level.

What is in This Chapter?

This chapter discusses what problems a board solves. Why would you want to form one, and why wouldn't you want to form one? How does a board impact the effectiveness and accountability of a company's management? Does forming a board mean that the owner/founder looses control of the company?

Do you remember those magic black eight ball toys? The one that looks like a huge billiard ball that you shake and then flip over to find an answer. Now imagine it held the answers to your questions about your business.

You grasp the eight ball in two hands, close your eyes. "Should I hire Bob as my new Vice President of Sales?" A quick shake and you flip it over to see the little blue window the answer 'yes' floating into view. You smile and go again, eyes closed. "Should I sign the contract with the new vendor to commit to buy 100,000 units?" A quick shake and you flip it over to see the answer, 'ask me again later'. Well, you can't win them all.

In many ways, a board of directors mirrors that magic eight ball. However, instead of getting a random answer you have the chance to tap into years of experience and get answers that will transform your business.

There are many good reasons to consider the formation of a fiduciary board and/or an advisory board. (More details are covered in the chapter *A Board of Directors vs. Advisory Board.*) There are however also a few risks. As the owner of a private company, how well you understand both, and move forward, can have a dramatic and material long-term effect on the success of your enterprise.

What Problem Does a Board Solve

What have you heard about boards of directors - officially known as fiduciary boards, as opposed to advisory boards? For most of those that own the controlling interest in a private company, the bulk of their knowledge comes from the business press in stories about the transitions or antics of large-cap public company boards; perhaps also an article here and there about board diversity.

Wow, what if I had a group of those?

Drew is the owner and CEO of a multi-million dollar manufacturer of very specialized electronic components – with over fifty patents. One day he was talking with the CEO of a large customer. The customer was highly satisfied with Drew's products and service and asked Drew to let him know if he could ever help him in any way. This was an unusual interaction for Drew, but he took a chance and mentioned that in fact he did have a problem. He told his customer that he was having trouble finding a reliable supplier of a particular item, and asked if he had any suggestions. The CEO offered to introduce Drew to his vendor for those items and invited Drew to accompany him to visit the vendor in China. The result was dramatic – higher quality, a lower price, and more reliable delivery. Well, this got Drew thinking. What if he could form a board comprised of several people who could give this kind of advice, make strategic introductions, and provide high-level guidance? This triggered him to start researching about the formation of a board.

There have been many evolutionary trends in American business over the last couple of decades. None has been more dramatic then the pressure on public companies - both regulatory and investor-driven - to upgrade their governance practices. Buried in these trends have also been private companies moving to emulate – where appropriate - the methods and governance processes of their larger public counterparts. This is being done for a number of reasons, both material and cosmetic or as they say in the technology sector, 'optics'.

But this begs the first question immediately asked by any company owner, "What problem does a board solve?" In firms profitable and not, with annual revenues from a few hundred thousand dollars to billions, they comment, "I am doing just fine without one." Understandable. They have their attorney, and their CPA, and even their fellow business-owner buddies at the country club. If one is ever willing to ask a question, or even share the truth of a situation with these 'colleagues' they are all willing to give their best advice - for free or for $250+ per hour.

An increasing number of private companies, especially growing and larger firms, are realizing that beyond the licensed legal and accounting advice, the general business counsel they are getting is not worth the price. I am not licensed to give legal advice, nor am I a CPA. However, being an attorney or accountant does not automatically qualify or 'license' one to give business advice. Direct experience is usually the only path to authority. Is it really the wisest choice to rely on your informal network, or even your attorney or accountant for advice on serious strategic issues in your unique industry?

A well-conceived, carefully assembled and balanced board can offer invaluable counsel on all that and more - far more valuable than the cost of maintaining the board.

There are many good reasons to form a board. Perhaps the most compelling is to strive to be a best-of-class example in your industry. Another, more basic reason, might be improving your company image in the eyes of customers, vendors, bankers, and even employees. From a practical standpoint, a board can be a valuable asset in preparing to raise capital or go public with an initial public offering (IPO).

One of the most important byproducts of a board is the increased accountability of management - whether or not that includes the owners. There is no leader of any business who does not ever make a mistake or an occasional error in judgment. Having a qualified board will dramatically reduce these and many other missteps. It gives even the most capable and experienced businessperson a key check and balance. When any decision is questioned by the board, it immediately raises a yellow flag, allowing management to reconsider based on the concerns of the board. Perhaps management was already aware of them, perhaps not. Regardless, this process reduces potential problems. In the end, the owner of the company may decide to stick to their original plan anyway, but they will certainly be more prepared and smarter for the process.

Aside from the governance aspects of a fiduciary board of directors, which a private company often does not require, there is the benefit of assembling a small group of true experts, at a relatively low cost. It gives an owner the opportunity to augment any weaknesses in high-level skill or experience without hiring another expensive full-time employee.

Could you use some fresh ideas? Has all your staff been with you for a long time? Is everyone strictly from your industry? A board director from another industry or business friend might be a source of innovative ideas. Do you have some tough competitors? A director that has dealt with those issues in another venue might be helpful. Would you like to acquire another company, or sell internationally, or outsource manufacturing to China but have not done it before? Your answer might be a board.

The right mix of directors can be a very practical solution when owners and their managers find that their personal experience in some critically important business areas is just not what it needs to be.

Why Would I Give up Control?

The most common response, to the need for a board, which I hear from the owners or management of any closely held company is "I don't want to give up control." We'll it's not about control – you do not sacrifice any. It's about knowing more, using your resources more wisely, and leveraging as much knowledge and experience as you possibly can. It's about working smarter and being smarter than your competition. A board is a strategic weapon. Perhaps even a nuclear one in your business' arsenal when wielded by wise management.

Let's take just a moment to understand the reporting dynamics of a board. A fiduciary board reports to the shareholders - or even the sole shareholder/owner - of the company. Their sole responsibility is to protect the interests of the ownership. One way or another all employees including senior management report to the CEO. The CEO in turn always reports to the board.

In the case where the CEO is not the sole or majority owner of the company, for example a large-cap public NYSE company, the reporting is very straight line - very simple. He or she can be directed and even fired by the board. But what about the case where the majority owner of the firm is the CEO? This creates a circular reporting structure, but still simple. The CEO reports to the board and the company ownership elects the board. Therefore, the board reports to the CEO. In the case of our CEO, the buck stops with him. As the owner he always has the final say. While the board provides him a platform for a critical analysis of his actions, and objective feedback, he can ultimately reject their views. If that makes them uncomfortable, their fiduciary and legal recourse is limited to their resignation.

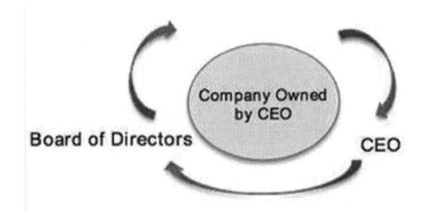

So, Why Take the Time and Spend the Money?

We have reviewed the upside of forming a board, but what is the downside?

If as the owner or one of the owners of a private enterprise, everything has been going very well, you might question the need for a board. If on the other hand things could have been better had you known more, or had you anticipated some of the things that have negatively impacted your company, or even if you had come up with that game changing innovation before your competitor did, then you should consider a board.

If it's that simple, then why not? For a start, forming a board in the first place, and managing and maintaining it, is very time consuming. Ultimately, it is the owners that undertake this task. If the owner and CEO are one in the same then where does the time come from? Like anything else, it has to be recognized as a priority. Yes, it will initially take valuable time away from your other management responsibilities. It is the board's potential for dramatically upping your company performance that makes it worth the trouble.

Another issue is cost. When forming a board for a privately owned company that intends to stay closely held, it is most often not desirable or feasible to compensate a board with equity, that is stock options or restricted stock. Of course you can consider some form of *phantom stock* or *synthetic equity*, but ultimately it boils down to paying the board in cash. I have seen small or early-stage private company board directors paid as little as $3,000 - $6,000 per year, depending on the amount and type of equity, if any. A company in the $250,000,000 range, with no real equity participation, should expect to pay directors $36,000 - $60,000. A larger enterprise may have to be competitive with public companies, which could range up to $250,000 per year.

In addition, there are usually additional fees paid to audit committee members and other committee chairmen. On top of the basic board fees there are travel expenses for attendance at meetings, the additional hard and soft costs of preparing board materials for meetings, and of course directors and officers insurance (D&O), which starts at least $5,000 per year (total, not per director) and goes up from there.

Yes, the biggest reason for not forming a board is the cost in management time, focus, and resources, and the monetary costs themselves. Beyond that forming a board is not for the thin-skinned. If you have well-qualified and experienced directors, they will be questioning your judgment. They will press you for your reasons and expectations at every turn. Their job is not to say how well you are doing, though they will, their job is to provide a counter balance to your thought process. They will push back on every choice you make, even if they agree. If you do not want anyone arguing with you (for the betterment of your enterprise of course), then pass. Lastly, another good reason for not pursuing a board is that you simply do not understand how they work and how the governance process in general is meant to build a stronger corporate infrastructure.

In my experience there are many reasons why talented and exceptionally successful people join a board. When recruiting directors I try to look beyond cash and equity to try to understand what other factors the candidate would find rewarding and compelling.

Back of the Envelope

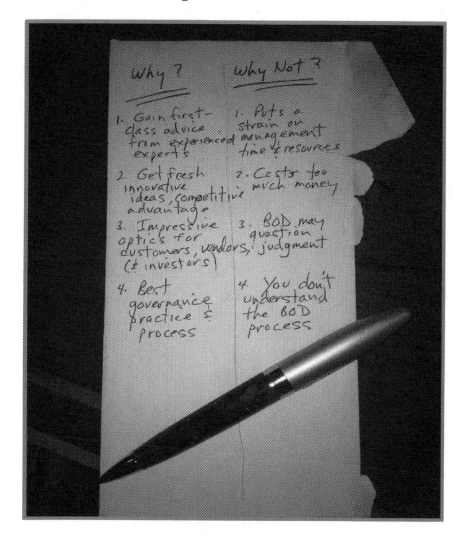

WHY?	WHY NOT?
1. Gain first-class advice from experienced experts	1. Puts a strain on management time & resources
2. Get fresh innovative ideas & competitive advantage	2. Costs too much money
3. Impressive optics for customers, vendors (& investors)	3. BOD may question your judgment
4. Best governance practices & process	4. You don't understand the BOD process

In Summary

In this chapter we have started with the problem a board solves, and why you should or should not form one. We covered how a board impacts the effectiveness and accountability of company management. Most importantly, we explored why forming a board does not necessarily sacrifice control of the company. The remainder of this book will answer most of your questions as it seeks to educate you on all the key facets of boards: fiduciary and advisory.

Chapter 2

A Board of Directors
vs. Advisory Board

Some CEOs and company owners don't think they need any outside advice, but most do. Everyone takes some counsel even if it's just our attorney, CPA or a close friend. For some, a board of directors can be a big step; and even if you already have one, it may not offer the diversity of experience and perspectives that a good business leader needs. An advisory board can make a business leader look very smart when used effectively.

What is in This Chapter?

This chapter discusses how a company can benefit from the advice of outside experts. You will learn the difference between an advisory board and a fiduciary board of directors, and some types of advisory boards. We will discuss the composition of boards and their value.

Today's business climate is more challenging than at any time in history. One of the byproducts of the Information Revolution in general, and mobile communications and the Internet in particular, is the compression of time and the ubiquity of information. There is more competition in every field, both domestically, and especially internationally. There are more regulations governing every aspect of industry, and in virtually every field there are multiple facets requiring increasingly specific experience and knowledge. The granularity of issues, business models and management specialties is overwhelming.

As the owner or CEO of any company, private or public, whether you already have a board of directors or not, an advisory board is an increasingly popular option for getting in-depth advice from a number of experts. If you do not already have a board of directors, and are not quite ready to take that step, an advisory board is a worthwhile consideration.

Advisors are specifically selected for their experience and skills as categorized by their knowledge of an industry vertical, their experience in a designated management discipline, or the economic sector they are from (e.g., government or education).

The three most common varieties of advisory boards are:

1. Those focused on prestige.
2. Those providing deep technical knowledge to augment the company's staff and provide credibility.
3. Those primarily selected to provide business development opportunities.

The determination of whether to form an advisory board (and which kind to form) is very subjective. If your firm is not required to have a board of directors, you could opt to just have advisors. If you are required to have directors, you could also add an advisory board.

An important step is to be able to clearly articulate the charter, or role, of either board. Establish clear objectives, standards, goals and tasks for the members. An important consideration is the bandwidth required of management to organize and manage the advisors. They need frequent attention to update them on company activities and solicit their contributions. Another consideration is the resources to compensate them; fees and/or equity. Also, does your company have the personnel and infrastructure to follow through on whatever advice, guidance or introductions a board member provides?

> ### What is fiduciary?
>
> A 'fiduciary' is an individual, corporation or association holding assets for another party, often with the legal authority and duty to make decisions regarding financial matters on behalf of the other party. Therefore a fiduciary board is a group of directors that collectively act as a fiduciary on behalf of the owners, shareholders or unit holders of a company. Thereby, the phrase 'the board has fiduciary responsibilities to the shareholders.'

The Key Difference

Although everyone may not always understand the differences between advisors and directors, and their uses may often overlap, there are some very important differences.

A board of directors, or board of managers for a LLC (Limited Liability Corporation) is a legal requirement for most corporate structures in most states. The corporate charters usually require them. Their purpose is governance and the oversight of management. They are hired/elected by the shareholders or unit holders, and owe their fiduciary responsibility to them. If a public company or a company with public debt they are legally empowered under the authority of the SEC and state corporate authorities, and must adhere to regulations like Sarbanes-Oxley.

Over the last ten or twenty years directors have faced increasing legal liability for their actions. These days any serious company, public or private, carries appropriate directors and officers (D&O) insurance coverage. One of the most frequent reasons given by qualified individuals for not accepting a director position - especially on a public board - is their concern about this liability.

In comparison, an advisory board is never a legal requirement, but rather simply engaged to advise the company. They have no liability or legal standing. They report to management and their primary purpose is providing the company with business and technical advice, contacts and business development opportunities, and credibility-by-association. Think consultants, but usually paid less.

Board Size and Meetings

Corporate charter and shareholder vote set the number of directors. There is really no standard or limit to the size of a well-formed advisory board. I have seen anywhere from one or two members up to thirty. The decision becomes a matter of how many individuals you can effectively manage without wasting your time or theirs. Also your budget for compensation will be a factor. In broadly held companies, particularly public ones, shareholders will want to seat a full board of directors, but with boards of directors for closely held firms, and with most advisory boards, you may start with a smaller number and add members as deemed appropriate.

While directors must hold a minimum of meetings, advisors may never actually need to meet as a group. The corporate charter and shareholder resolutions will determine the number of board meetings. Although usually a minimum number must be held in person, telephonic or video conference calls can be acceptable for others. Most of the boards of directors I have sat on met monthly. Many of these met once each quarter in person and the others by telephone. Just as there is rarely any advisory board voting, there are often few meetings.

The individual contributor nature of advisors lends itself to management often engaging with most advisors on a one-to-one basis. With the advisors there is no overriding need to assemble in total. But, unless you are doing it for pure show and public relations, which will wear thin quickly, especially with your advisors, you will want to actually meet. The nature of the advisory board may be such that twice a year might work; on the other hand, it could also be a monthly schedule including some in-person as a group and some individually on the phone.

The most important reason for an all-advisor meeting is to be able to brainstorm on larger overreaching strategic issues as a team. It can often create a great deal of intellectual leverage. This is not to say that advisory board group meetings are not productive, if only once or twice a year. It's often easier to update them all on the state of the business at the same time. Also, the collective brainstorming and enthusiastic interaction of the full mix of assembled experience and perspective can be incredibly productive, especially from a strategic standpoint. It's not uncommon to make a periodic advisory board meeting a milestone event for management and key employees to prepare for and present to.

Composition

In small and private companies, the board of directors serves the shareholders, particularly controlling shareholders. Advisors on the other hand serve management, not the board or shareholders, unless they are one in the same. Their sole function is to provide management with advice and counsel: strategic and tactical, and business connections.

Advisors are selected for specific expertise including deeper industry and technical knowledge, and a robust contact database. They augment management's perspective on business issues: general business, industry specific, technical, and regulatory; and also provide deeper expertise in skills like sales, marketing, finance, legal, manufacturing, R&D, logistics, and international. Ultimately, the selection of your board members will simply boil down to the best people you can meet and convince to serve. However, it can be very helpful to start off more strategically with a wish list of characteristics and prospects.

The most desirable characteristics vary for directors and advisors, given the differences in purpose. Advisors main job is advice and counsel, as opposed to directors, whose main job is governance. Advisors can have overlapping skills since there is really no limit to the number you can have. There are some good arguments for seating some people of great stature on advisory boards, especially when they also possess the complimentary skills and expertise that you are looking for.

In fact, some very high-profile people would prefer to join as an advisor rather than a director (less liability, less pressure, less structure, less time, less ... serious).

What personalities make the best advisors? Truthfully? Any. One might wonder how these two different boards might interact. Frankly, I have never seen them meet each other. Directors may be updated by management on the activities of the advisors, but the advisors rarely are privy to anything going on with the directors.

Board of Directors

Try for individuals with at least one characteristic
from each column (selected examples only)

CEO	Big company/organization
CFO	Your industry
Sales	Technology
Marketing	Large customer/vendor/strategic partner
Government/political/regulatory	International
Non-profit	Manufacturing
Academic	Legal

Advisory Board

An individual with any one characteristic relating to your business is good.

Current or past executives (not necessarily C-level)
Past government officials
Science – multiple relevant disciplines
Technology – multiple relevant areas
Notable customers
Key vendors
Important strategic partner(s)

FUNCTION COMPARISON		
	Board of Directors	**Advisory Board**
Governance Responsibility	YES	NO
Legal Liability	YES	NO
Reports To	Shareholders, by annual vote	Management, usually hired under consulting agreement
Regulatory Authority	SEC, State, SOX, corp. charter	Management under authority of BOD
General Business Advice	YES, but structured for governance	YES, structured only for individuals advising management in their areas of specific expertise
Typical Number of Members & Format	Workable size designed to function as a coordinated group: 3-7	Based only on the need for advice in very well defined domains of expertise, not necessarily in any coordinated group: 2-25
Weighted Toward	Judgment-experience-respect, fiduciary responsibilities to shareholders, higher level issues, management considerations, internal operations, capital, and macro-trends	Meaningful strategic/tactical business advice, more detailed issues related to individual expertise like business development, technology or industry knowledge
Meetings/Time Required	Formal format (Robert's), in-person preferred but some by phone acceptable: 4-12/yr., requires constant attention and regular time commitment	No standards, sometimes infrequent group meetings but usually only individually and often only by phone: 1-6/yr., time varies widely but is only on-demand
Skills Focus	CEO's, financial, sales, marketing, manufacturing, academic, government, legal, notoriety	Technology, science, vertical industry, big company execs
Optics	Prestige is important, but not without substance these days; judgment, experience, credibility are key	Name recognition sometimes is main criteria, but unique deep domain knowledge should be key, with ability to help in very specific ways

Compensation

It is unlikely that anyone of substance will serve on an advisory board without compensation. Advisory fees vary widely depending on the size of the company and the demand for the advisor's expertise. Compensation is covered in more detail in a later chapter.

Fees can be fixed when based on a relatively fixed time commitment, or variable based on the number of meetings, calls, or assigned tasks. Compensation can be cash, equity, or a combination of both. The cash fee can be a monthly or annual retainer, or variable, for example per meeting. An equity component is almost always present, usually in the form of a non-qualified option grant.

Amounts vary widely but are usually set relative to (and below) the level of equity options for senior management and the board. Although most advisors will service for a modest annual retainer and some options, others are more expensive. For example, professional consultants, in particular, will not usually serve at a substantial discount from their usual fees. A reasonable general rule of thumb is to target advisor compensation at approximately one half of the lowest compensated director. You may designate someone to lead your advisory board, which would warrant additional pay. A later chapter on Compensation Models and Metrics will cover this in more detail.

In Summary

Both fiduciary and advisory boards are wonderful tools to enlist the counsel of prestigious and knowledgeable individuals, on a very wide variety of issues. If you can afford the time and compensation there is no real limit to the number. They can provide the best possible in-depth advice, at the lowest overall cost, about your business, markets, industry, competition, customers, sector, products, technology, and much more. Be prepared to consult with them frequently, but not necessarily collectively. At any point you wish, you can easily terminate or replace an advisor, or even the entire advisory board for that matter. Advisors and directors are both incredible assets to a company and its senior management. They can provide a business leader with a competitive advantage, and when used effectively, make them look very smart.

Chapter 3

Finding Directors

Don't be shy in your recruiting efforts. This can be a fun and educational experience. The dynamics of forming a board of directors for a private or early-stage company are complex, and entrepreneurs often fail to understand, or appreciate, the uses and risks of boards. Getting started is often about recruiting the right people and balancing their skills.

What is in This Chapter?

This chapter discusses a number of things to consider before recruiting board members (or directors). You will read how to identify qualified prospects and how to take the first step toward attracting them to your board. Finally, read how to convince them to serve and close the deal.

As the owner or CEO of a private company the question may arise about the benefits of forming a board of directors. As a businessperson you may have read articles or books about boards. These are usually about large Fortune 500 companies, and cover specific topics, such as governance, compensation and sometimes their inappropriate behavior. But if you have a private company, or an early-stage company - especially one that is smaller and not in the Fortune 1,000 category - where do you start?

There are an abundance of issues around forming a board: the risks and benefits, how to form it, and what to do with it after it's formed. However, perhaps the most important consideration is who the actual directors will be and what value they add to your business.

Board Considerations

The board's primary job is to give management good advice, surfacing all the pertinent issues for your consideration and open discussion, and providing you with the benefit of their broader, and perhaps deeper, experience. The second job is to lend their name and credibility to the company, usually for purposes of building credibility with customers, vendors, employees, and of course investors.

Stakeholders and business partners feel a greater sense of confidence knowing that a company's ownership and leadership solicits and values the advice of outside professionals. With these objectives in mind, the most important consideration at the outset is who the actual directors will be.

> *"Personalities are good, everyone should have one, but on a board they need to be held in check so as to allow each person to give their best advice..."*

The process for defining the 'who' must take into consideration the board members' individual and collective core skills, experience, as well as their ability to drive results to your bottom-line. Perhaps one of the least appreciated skills needed by directors is how they communicate and work within a team. A room full of high-powered, big-name, big-ego CEOs, venture capitalists, retired businessmen, or private equity folks are not going to provide one bit of value-added advice if they cannot relate to your company management and ownership and communicate with others effectively.

Personalities are good; everyone should have one. But on a board they need to be held in check so as to allow each person to give their best advice, in the most constructive way, and not go overboard in either being too agreeable for the sake of perceived unanimity or stubborn obstruction when they are not in the majority.

You might be thinking, "That's all great, but I don't even know anyone who has ever been on a board, or anyone who has a notable reputation. Where am I going to ever find someone qualified, and convince them to serve?"

Identifying Your Prospects

One thing to keep in mind is that we all know other smart, experienced folks - whether through our schooling, professional career, hobbies, mutual friends, or organizations. There are few set requirements for a director. In starting out, it is about getting the best possible people you can recruit.

It's worth noting that directors are not elected for life. Over time you will meet new people that may be even more successful, experienced and noteworthy. As your company grows there is nothing wrong with upgrading your directors individually. There are sensitive ways to replace directors, and any director should understand and respond professionally to your request.

The First Step

The first step is very simple. The search starts by simply compiling a list of possible candidates, and people you know who might be able to recommend others. Add to your list people you may have heard of in business and whom you respect and admire. It does not necessarily matter how well you know them. Successful people will have good personal networks, and most likely they are respected and admired. They could be the source of good referrals, even if they are not interested themselves.

In addition to candidates you know personally, you can also ask for leads and introductions from your banker, attorney, accountant, other business owners or CEOs you know. Good sources can include a pastor or rabbi, relatives in business and family friends. Although you may already be acquainted with some of these people, you should be equally open to good suggestions of prospects that you may have not yet met. Explain to all of these key contacts what you are looking for and actively solicit their suggestions for board members.

In building your board, it is worthwhile to have a good idea of the key skill sets and experience that you feel would augment and compliment your own, and those of your management team. Could your firm benefit from more depth in sales, marketing or operations? How do you stack up in finance, international business, or technology? Could your firm use the perspective of the opposite sex? Could someone who is an expert in manufacturing, retailing, healthcare, government relations, information technology, or travel add to your perspective on your business marketplace or operations?

Regardless, compile your list of desirable attributes. Strategize those areas that you would like represented and target them in your interviews.

Convincing Them to Serve

Once you have your list with a good number of possible board candidates, it's time to start the interview process. Don't be shy. This can be a fun and educational experience. You may consider yourself too reserved to be calling these people cold. Don't worry. It has never been easier to reach out and establish contact in business. People have never been more open to meeting you and expanding their own networks. It is always considered an honor to be interviewed to join a board of directors.

Of course the best start is an introduction from a mutual contact, but with the advancement of social media and tools such as LinkedIn, Facebook, Google, and email (to name just a few), it has never been easier, or more acceptable, to proactively introduce yourself to others. Even if they are not interested or ultimately are not a fit, just reaching out may help your business in ways that you could not imagine.

A Big Catch

A number of years ago I was searching for a high-level director for a high-technology company that I had co-founded. I hoped for someone truly exceptional, both for their contribution and their credibility. I heard around town that Tom Everhart, a retired professor, was living nearby. I checked him out by asking around and researching on the Internet. He had been a noted scientist and the president of one of the country's most respected technical universities. I was able to obtain his email address (not that hard these days), and I sent a polite invitation to get together over lunch to get to know one another. He accepted and we met several times. Finally, I asked whether he would consider joining our board. He respectfully declined stating that he was too busy with the other boards he was then on (General Motors, Raytheon, Hewlett Packard and Hughes Aircraft - wow!). I countered with an invitation to join our advisory board instead: fewer meetings, less responsibility, no liability. Tom was intrigued with what we were doing and liked our team, so he accepted. A few years later he retired from those big boards and joined our board of directors. Over the years, I have learned a tremendous amount from this gentleman.

Interviewing these high achievers is much like interviewing prospective employees, except that generally you can learn even more from them. It's an opportunity to get to know them and ask them any number of questions that will give you valuable business knowledge, and also indicate the way they think. You can often learn more about them from the questions they ask you then the ones you ask them.

This process is very interactive. In addition to qualifying them, you also need to sell them. Not only will you want to pick the best directors, but also they will need to be sold on you and your company. In order to get an acceptance, you will need to tap one or more motivating interests of that person.

- Do they like you personally and want to help?
- Are they fascinated by your business?
- Do they find your challenges stimulating?
- Do they feel that they can materially contribute and add value to your enterprise?

Who the other board members are will often make a difference as well. Directors like to engage with others that they can enjoy and learn from. It's like playing tennis; you won't improve unless you play with better players.

Long ago, I developed my personal checklist for joining a board. My considerations are: who else is on the board, what business is the company in, is the company properly funded, where are they located, and what is the compensation for directors (does it balance the liability)?

Compensation

What about that tricky issue, compensation?

First of all, realize that it is not all about the money at this level. No one is going to expect your firm to pay directors $250,000 or more. They might not even expect a large stock option grant, especially if it is closely held with no outside investors and has no aspirations of a liquidity event.

What will it take then?

It will need to be something that satisfies each prospect, and be in addition to the qualitative benefits of fellowship, learning experience, and personal satisfaction. To some extent compensation will also depend on how many directors you have and how many of them are compensated. You may have one or two company managers or owners, including yourself, on the board. You should not have more. Owners or employees usually are not paid to be on the board. You can start adding directors one at a time; there is no reason to hurry. In most situations, a five- or seven-person board is probably going to work best. In the end, it is important that the compensation for all paid directors should be somewhat consistent, with perhaps a little more for key committee chairs (like finance).

There is a wide range of compensation alternatives. The choices include a monthly or per meeting cash stipend, stock options, restricted stock, profit sharing, bonus based on company performance, and more. Usually, some combination of these will do the trick. The magnitude of each depends specifically on your company size, development stage, financial condition and precedent within your peer group or industry.

In Summary

Many entrepreneurs fail to appreciate both the benefits and risks of a board. Some get their first lesson when new investors impose one on them. I don't advise waiting, but rather take the initiative and form one comprised of your selections. Use its strength and knowledge to accelerate your company's success. Don't worry about 'leaving room' for an investor; they will always take care of themselves. Take the action to recruit a board of directors whom you respect, admire, and trust. Get the advantage of this important and powerful governance tool now.

Chapter 4

Questions: What to Ask Director Candidates, and What They Will Ask You

Interviewing candidates for a board of directors is a very specific process. Not too dissimilar from interviewing a prospective CEO, it involves evaluating a wide variety of criteria, and at the same time educating the candidate, and convincing them of why they should join your company – should they ultimately be invited. However, there is one fundamental difference between interviewing someone for an executive position as opposed to a board directorship.

What is in This Chapter?

This chapter addresses the process of selecting and interviewing director candidates. It gives an overview of some questions to ask them, and some of the questions they might be asking you. Most importantly, are they both qualified and suitable to be on your board?

When interviewing a candidate for a senior executive role he or she will most likely be a subordinate, or a peer, but nonetheless an employee. Personal chemistry and cultural fit within the company are of course very important. However, a director is not an employee, nor is he/she necessarily a peer. They could potentially exceed the CEOs own level of accomplishment in one area or another, and it is not always mandatory that they are a good fit with the company culture but it is desirable.

In general, they will not be working side-by-side, or socializing with employees. That said they are required to understand, appreciate, and respect the company culture. On the other hand, the culture of the board, their personalities, and the dynamics between the directors, is critical. The board chairman, the lead or presiding director, a member of the nominating or governance committee, the CEO, or any combination of these will usually conduct board interviews.

Qualified vs. Suitable

The chances are that you would not even be spending the time to meet with a board candidate unless they came highly recommended, and with confirmed impressive credentials. Keep in mind that qualifications and suitability are two very different considerations. They are both part objective, but also part subjective.

Qualifications will help you rate their experience, success, achievements, levels of responsibilities and exposure to a requisite range of circumstances that would benefit your company. Suitability is somewhat more empirical. It represents the person's potential chemistry with the other board members, and stakeholders like management, ownership, and outside consultants.

How do you judge their personality and style that will enable them to actively participate and provide their professional advice, while being respectful of the time and opinions of others? Basically, are they capable of playing in the same sandbox with other high-level, high-energy, highly accomplished individuals, or are they really best when playing alone where they are always in charge?

Once you arrive at a selection of candidates, who meet the level of qualification you require, in terms of skills and experience, you should further sort based on personalities that will fit well with the culture you seek to develop for the board itself, and the existing or desired company culture. There is always a risk when you assemble a group of five or ten hi-performance high-achievement dynamic Type-A individuals. Warning: the degree to which anyone does not exhibit professionalism, control, and rationality, and makes the issue or discussion about them and not about the best interests of the company, will quickly shift the board away from being an asset, to being a liability.

Interviewing Process

This interviewing process is always half about you asking all of your questions, but it is also importantly about the questions the candidate asks you. Do they maintain an appropriate balance between the completeness and brevity of their answers, the style and personality they exhibit when answering, and the delicate ratio between talking about themselves vs. drawing you out?

This document is not intended to provide any insight into the correct answers to any questions – there are no set answers. Rather, it is to help (a) guide your thinking toward a selection of questions that have traditionally provided the range and depth of information necessary to be able to evaluate a person's qualifications and suitability, and (b) to prepare you to answer a representative sample of some of the questions most frequently asked by prospective board members.

Be prepared to listen to the candidate's answers thoughtfully and control the direction you want the meeting to go in by drilling down on subjects you want more information on, and gently guiding the interview away from those that do not benefit your selection in some way.

If you want to attract the best talent be prepared to answer their questions in a straightforward, accurate and candid way. One of the most desirable attributes of a world-class director is their ability to hone in and ask the tough questions. Use the candidate's questions themselves to understand and evaluate the depth of their knowledge, their understanding of your business, their analytical and strategic skills, and how well they would mix with the personal chemistry of your other directors, the company shareholders/owners and the management team. You can often learn more from the questions they ask than the answers they give to your questions. Remember you are looking for someone who has the ability to think in a manner that is different to you. A person that can push you hard to justify the rationale behind your thought process and decision making.

These questions are not arranged in any order. In fact, regardless of the order the individual should be able to track them and focus on giving you the information you are asking for. Please note that I recommend asking these questions with respect, not quite as bluntly as they are stated below. Also, whenever possible I try to lead candidates to reveal all this information without ever directly asking them the questions. This creates a much smoother cadence to the encounter and a much better basis for actually beginning to develop a relationship, which is important if they are selected, and is more problematic when it comes off like an interrogation.

One important cautionary note; beware of a candidate that won't stop talking, even in answer to one of your questions. This is a red flag that they may be prone to wanting to dominate conversation in the boardroom, which is not appropriate. Lastly, I usually recommend trying to keep a good balance between asking questions and answering their questions. Although I have done interviews where I found it better to answer all the candidate's questions first, then simply ask the few remaining questions that did not get covered in the course of the conversation.

The following questions represent a sample of some of the questions most frequently asked of and by director candidates.

Questions for a Prospective Board Director:

- ☐ *What are your personal objectives or goals for a board, and your expectations for a director?*
- ☐ *What would you suggest your unique contribution to be?*
- ☐ *What are your objectives or goals for joining a Board, and your expectations for a director?*
- ☐ *What are your personal criteria for joining a board (presumably beyond just being invited)?*
- ☐ *What do you already know about our company?*
- ☐ *What other boards are you currently on or have previously been on?*
- ☐ *What were some of the most interesting experiences you have had related to boards, and some of the most important things you have learned?*
- ☐ *What do you feel were some of your greatest contributions?*
- ☐ *Were you ever considered for a board and not selected?*
- ☐ *What are you currently doing professionally (active in a company, retired, etc.)?*
- ☐ *Give us a brief chronology of your career over time.*
- ☐ *What do you consider to be your core area(s) of expertise?*
- ☐ *What kind of time commitments do you now have for your current activities?*
- ☐ *What would your expectations be for the time necessary for our board?*
- ☐ *Who are some of the most notable people you have worked with or served on boards with?*
- ☐ *What board committee would you see yourself most/least qualified for?*
- ☐ *What is your expectation for the compensation package for directors?*

- ❑ *Tell us a little about your upbringing and your family.*
- ❑ *What extracurricular or outside interest do you have?*
- ❑ *What is the most difficult problem and decision that a board you have been on has had to deal with?*
- ❑ *How would you deal with a difficult board member who you do not agree with?*
- ❑ *What business failures have you had that you learned the most from that might benefit our company?*
- ❑ *What other questions do you have for us that we have not answered?*

Questions from A Prospective Board Director:

- ❑ What are your objectives or goals for the Board, and your expectations for a director?
- ❑ What would you expect my unique contribution to be? What would you want from me?
- ❑ What are the structural details of the company including incorporation (type, state), how long in business, fully diluted ownership (capital schedule), etc.?
- ❑ What are revenues/profits, and how are they broken out – by product, business unit, geography, etc.?
- ❑ Explain the business you are in.
- ❑ How and where do you actually make your profits?
- ❑ Who are your customers – where does the money come from?
- ❑ What are the key drivers/economic levers for the business – capital, labor, IP, products, cost structure, etc.?
- ❑ What are the most significant riskes that could negatively affect your business?
- ❑ Fill me in on the operational details such as annual revenue, profit margins, number of employees, facilities, corporate entities, creation of products and services, capital requirements, competition, etc.

❑ How much of my time will be required – for pre and interim-meeting preparation, and for meetings (board, committee, employee, etc.)?

❑ Who else is on (or going to be on) the Board? What is the anticipated size of the Board, and the balance between inside and outside Directors?

❑ Who is chairman and/or lead director?

❑ Who are your key executives, their tenure and backgrounds, and their compensation?

❑ What is the compensation package for directors?

❑ Is D&O (Directors & Officers) Insurance in place, what are the limits? Please provide a full copy with all riders.

❑ What questions have other candidates asked that I have not, yet?

In Summary

Picking and interviewing board members is a lot like when you were a child and chose up teams for kickball or dodge ball. You wanted the best players on your team, but they also had to be team players, not showboats. You sensitively yet effectively interview them, asking them your questions. Woven into that process is giving them truthful, meaningful and compelling answers to their questions. In the end you need to convince them to want to join your team; then you decide if you want them.

Chapter 5

Forming a Private Company's First Fiduciary Board: Step-By-Step

The first time formation of a fiduciary board of directors involves a somewhat more complicated process than simply filling a board seat on an already existing board. The formation of a board for a private company can also vary in certain ways from the formation of a public company board. Here is a high-level view of some of the important elements necessary to form a board, arranged in a simple critical path format.

What is in This Chapter?

This chapter is the solid meat and potatoes of forming a board. Just like a kitchen recipe, it walks you through twenty-nine definitive steps – one by one. It starts with proper incorporation and ends with listing your board members' bios on your website. Included are reviews of an LLC vs C corporation, and D&O insurance.

A client recently retained me to educate him on considering whether or not to install a fiduciary board of directors. This young man had founded a high-technology company and still owned controlling interest; he was no longer active in management, however his minority partner was the CEO. The company was over one hundred million in revenue, and being very smart, analytical and inquisitive he asked me, "How do you actually form a board." Although I had explained this many times, he wanted it from me in writing, and with a flow chart no less.

Well, there are a myriad of considerations for a private company, where do you start? Certainly you know people, and you even know some people who know some people. Do you just ask? What about your corporate documentation? Are you even properly incorporated? How do you determine what skills you need? Here are the basics.

Step-By-Step

This article will go through twenty-nine steps leading up to conducting your first board meeting. Many of these steps can be undertaken in parallel. One could undoubtedly come up with other points, and variations of these, but these basics will get you through the basics.

1. Incorporate in an appropriate entity (C or LLC).
It is becoming much more common for privately owned enterprises to want to take advantage of the tremendous value-addition that a top-flight board can provide. Even those that do not envision an eventual exit by way of an initial public offering or acquisition are forming fiduciary boards. In order to have a legal fiduciary board of directors (board), the company must have a corporate structure, as opposed to a partnership. Typically, it would be a C corporation, especially if a sale or public offering is envisioned eventually. However, an LLC (limited liability corporation) may also have a board, although the structure and implementation are much less well defined by corporate case law (see sidebar below).

2. Gain the consensus of majority of ownership and decide if a board is appropriate for your company.
The formation of a board can initiate a very positive chain of events. Those outside the company – customers, vendors, strategic partners, competitors, bankers, investors, etc. - will view the firm differently, usually as more professional and better managed. Inside

the company, employees will also sense a difference and tend to feel that the company is more serious and respectable. However, with all the benefits and dividends that a board can provide, it can be problematic without the full support of ownership.

Of course it is possible, depending on the details of a company's shareholders agreements and structure, that a simple majority of ownership could establish a board. However, the outcome is much more likely to result in all the positives if the move has the support of all the owners. With a private company, moving to seat a board always brings up issues of potential loss of control. While fundamentally this is not the case, the perception still lingers and can create discord and contention. I would rarely recommend the creation of a board unless an overwhelming majority of ownership endorses the concept.

LLC vs. C Corporation

Laws in every state require that a corporation have a board of directors elected by the shareholders. An LLC (limited liability corporation) does have some of the same characteristics as a corporation, however they are not required to have a board of directors. Rather, in most states, the regulations allow an optional board if the members (owners) so choose. This governance arrangement would be part of the document filed to create the LLC, typically known as a Certificate of Organization, Articles of Organization, or Operating Agreement. Articles of Organization must designate which of two types of management structures the company will have – it will either be Manager-managed, or Member-managed. Manager-managed means that the power and authority of the company's management rests with the Board of Managers, which is similar to the Board of Directors of a Corporation. If Member-managed the LLC has no Board of Managers, and is managed by its members (owners), with authority in proportion to their ownership. Both structures are good but serve different long-term objectives, and have varying tax consequences.

Formation of a New Fiduciary Board of Directors: Critical Path

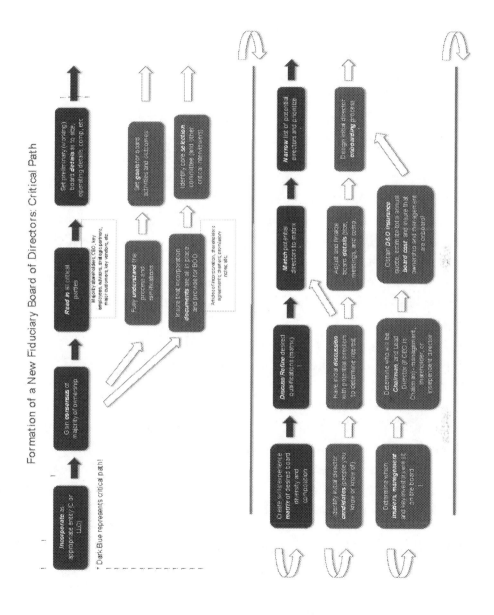

3. Brief all key parties on the plan to form a board, including a clear majority of shareholders (if closely held), the CEO, other key employees, advisors, and if appropriate strategic partners, major customers, key vendors, etc.

Once the key owners, or a decisive majority of them, have made this decision to form a board, it is helpful to engage a broader audience. This should by no means involve 'everyone', but simply 'key' stakeholdetrs. The company's C-level management, if it is not already part of ownership, your attorney, accountant, primary banker (especially if you have any debt), and possibly even some key customers or strategic partners.

This has several benefits. First, you begin to build your company's credibility and respect even before the board is actually organized. Second, this select group of close 'friends of the firm' could well have some insights that might be helpful, and they may have some recommendations for director candidates. You should begin your list of potential directors as soon as possible, and with the most desirable and qualified candidates possible.

4. Fully understand the process and ramifications of a board.

Of course all the details of forming and administering a board will affect the final decision on whether or not to have one. However, it is not necessary to understand all this unless the owners fundamentally agree that they want one. Considerations such as time commitment, cost, politics, governance impact, legal liabilities, etc. will come into play. Generally, these do not really change someone's mind, but should be fully understood at this stage regardless.

5. Set goals for board activities and outcomes.

As with any corporate undertaking there are expectations to manage and results to be measured. It is no different with a board. I am not reviewing examples of board goals here, however without articulating and documenting them it is harder to communicate with stakeholders, including potential directors, and the results of your recruiting and board activities as a whole will be far less satisfactory. The best goals have to do with improving the company's performance and enterprise value, however even something as simple as needing a qualified fiduciary board to fulfill SOX compliance for an eventual IPO is valid.

6. Insure that incorporation documents are all in place and provide for a board, including articles of incorporation, shareholders' agreements, charters, promissory notes, etc.

Too many times I have seen this step short-changed. When the documentation is not in order on the front end, it leads to confusion, discontent and wasting substantial time. Worse results can include inadvertent illegality, lawsuits and at worse abandoned M&A or financing transactions. Make sure you have properly established the necessary incorporation structure. Take the time to create or restate the Articles of Incorporation (or Organization).

The document(s) needs to include proper designation for a board, the number of directors, the term and other similar elections. It is not unheard of for errors in these to go undetected for years, only to surface in the middle of an important transaction – like selling the company or an IPO. It is unlikely to derail a deal, but it does add a loss of confidence and substantial delays when the buyer or an investment banker points out that the board did not in fact have the legal authority to approve the deal. All this will surface during due diligence and could even result in a reduced valuation.

7. Set the preliminary board details such as size, operating details and compensation.

Please note that I say preliminary. These details can change before the board is fully seated, and thereafter. There is no one – or even best – model here. It is very subjective, but there are some hints that will keep options open going forward. Set some parameters rather than fixed numbers, e.g. authorize for nine directors, but with the intention of only having five to seven to start; plan on meetings every month to six weeks, with two out of three by phone and the third in person; or peg the compensation within a reasonable dollar range, but do not fix it until the board meets (allow for equity or profit sharing options, but don't fix the form or amount). It is not mandatory that all potential issues be covered up front. Experienced directors will tolerate the ambiguity and help walk the management through the process.

8. Create a skills/experience matrix of the desired board diversity and composition.

Start by looking objectively at the horizontal and vertical (domain) skill set and experience of the management team. Look also at the major potential risks and potential for the firm. Then consider, in light of these risks and rewards, which talent, experience and skills, are the most needed and in the shortest supply within your existing team. These are part of the basis for your matrix. Add to that the traditional best-of-class items that might strengthen your roster, e.g. qualified financial expert, highly regarded former CEO, noted industry or academic authority, etc. This creates a somewhat objective basis on which to compare and balance candidates to form the most diverse and relevant board you can.

9. Identify initial director candidates. These are people who are known directly or recommended.

So often I talk to owners or managers who don't know where to start. Just start writing down names. Who do you or your colleagues know, or simply know of, that might be a potential candidate. Ask your trusted advisors like your attorney or accounting firm for recommendations. Build your list. (Note: see my article Finding directors for the smaller and early-stage company, *Directors & Boards Magazine*, Second Quarter 2012.)

Do not be timid in exploring a variety of sources for your candidates. Call industry leaders. Check with industry associations. Use LinkedIn to its fullest potential. Call colleagues at other companies, in other industries, in other geographies. Talk with leadership at local University business schools, or your own alma mater.

Be creative, perhaps a senior executive recently retired from a significant competitor, or some other industry figure, and they don't have any anti-competitive restrictions. Reach far and wide in your initial thinking. If there is a specific skill set that would really make a big difference, search for it. Executive search firms that recruit directors are very good. However, I have never found it necessary to use one. It is always more compelling for a director to be solicited by a member of the ownership or the CEO, then an outsider.

10. Identify the core selection committee. Also identify others who are critical to include in the interviewing process.
Who is going to make **the** decision on who gets invited to join the board? Whose input will be important, even if they do not necessarily get a vote? Who will take the lead in the process of contacting the prospects, reaching out to them, informing them of the opportunity, initially convincing them to consider it, and collecting their relevant personal information and questions?

Choose carefully since this individual is the first person they will build their impression of the firm on. A fumbled approach can cost a potentially valuable director. Remember that often the best you could get will be the hardest to recruit.

11. Have an initial discussion with all potential directors to determine interest.
After your list is refined, and ranked by preference, reach out. There is a balance here. It is very productive to meet as many of these folks as possible, yet it is time consuming and you don't want to set any false expectations. The process of meeting a highly qualified group like this can be fun, stimulating and educational.

Don't short-change the benefits. It is advisable to have your proposed engagement well prepared. Be ready to give them the key points of your request and simply determine their interest and availability. Can they afford the time, and are they interested in talking further? That's it for now.

12. Refine the matrix of desired qualifications.
After initially talking with the candidates you have identified, consider their qualifications and re-examine the best potential mix to gain maximum board diversity across all the critical areas. If necessary, refine your matrix based on any new knowledge or awareness.

13. Determine which insiders, management and key investors will sit (or not sit) on the board.
Now that you have seen some candidates, and had time to think about a board, it is time to begin to nail down who among the existing stakeholders should actually sit as a director. Keep in mind that key executives below the CEO can attend meetings and give the board their input, but do not necessarily have to have a vote.

- *If there are co-founders, should they all sit on the board regardless of management position or equity percentage?*
- *Was anyone promised a directorship?*
- *Is there any preferred series of stock that needs or is required to have board representation?*
- *Is there a key investor or advisor that is so valued and respected that you want their balance on the board?*

All said, a best-of-class fiduciary board of directors should have a majority of independent directors – those not employed by the company, or with major equity or other potential conflicts of interest. Although this certainly is not a mandatory requirement for private companies, it is best practice. Yet still, three inside (employees or major equity holders) and four outside is an excellent benchmark for starting out.

14. Determine who will be Chairman, and Lead Director (if CEO is Chairman): management, shareholder, or independent director.
The board will need a chairman. Normally the board would elect one, however in a private enterprise it is more common for the primary owners to determine whom this should be. It could be the majority owner or their designee. It could be the original founder, the CEO, or an experienced outsider. Who has the experience to do it, or who wants to fill the position and learn the ropes?

If an insider is chairman, then best practices dictate the election or appointment of a presiding director, or also termed, lead director. If a less experienced insider were chairman, then it would be to their benefit to have a more seasoned presiding director to back them up. There are duties involved. There is time involved. There is leadership and political considerations (even in an extremely cordial environment).

15. Match the list of potential directors to the qualifications.
The narrowing down process continues. Match up all the players, rank them by preference, categorize their skills, compare qualifications against your matrix, and sort and shuffle.

16. Adjust the qualifications, if necessary, and finalize board details. Make your final determination as to size.
Continue the previous step to a conclusion. Make the final decision on size based on your view of the process and candidates at this time. It can be changed later.

I recommend initially authorizing more seats, filling the ones you feel good about, and planning on adding more folks later as you get a better understanding of your needs and dynamics. For example, authorize for nine, seat three management/ownership, and four independents. If anyone does not work out you can always ask someone to leave and reduce to six. If you feel that you could use more expertise in a particular area, or you simply meet a dynamite person, you can add one to have eight. It is flexible and does not have to be an odd number.

I believe in slightly more board diversity and balance, as opposed to keeping the board small. A good chairman or presiding director will manage the process and keep the wheels of governance greased.

17. Obtain D&O insurance quote, estimate total annual board cost, and insure that ownership and management are onboard.
This step involves determining the entire overall monetary cost of having a board. This primarily includes the cash fees paid to directors. Typically, only independent directors draw a fee. There is the base board fee, plus add-ons for committee assignments, special committees and other increases in time, responsibility and liability. There are also T&E expenses for director travel related to their role. In addition, there may be slightly increased legal or accounting costs related to both meetings and special reporting associated with board oversight.

The time and cost of preparing for board meetings and making board arrangements is real, but it is usually absorbed in other administrative positions. A significant annual cost is Directors and Officers (D&O) insurance. It is very important to obtain this in the beginning. The limits vary and the fees vary accordingly. Poll your directors and corporate counsel to determine the best balance between coverage and fees based on the combined perceived liabilities and risks.

> ## Directors and Officers Liability Insurance
>
> *Directors and officers liability insurance (usually referred to as D&O) is liability insurance payable to the directors and officers of a company, or to the organization(s) itself, as indemnification (reimbursement) for losses or advancement of defense costs in the event an insured suffers such a loss as a result of a legal action brought for alleged wrongful acts in their capacity as directors and officers. Such coverage can extend to defense costs arising out of criminal and regulatory investigations/trials as well; in fact, often civil and criminal actions are brought against directors/officers simultaneously. Intentional illegal acts, however, are typically not covered under D&O policies.*

18. Design initial director on-boarding process.

In large part, the value of your board will be based on their in depth understanding of your business. You cannot assume that they will start off knowing much about it. In order to derive the maximum benefit as soon as possible, it is important to have a somewhat formalized 'on-boarding' process. This is best when not done ad hoc, but rather thoughtfully designed and planned.

On-boarding is typically comprised of some combination of written materials, educational sessions, meetings with key company personnel, visits to company facilities, and perhaps even meetings or conversations with key company customers, vendors, financiers, consultants, counselors, etc. The length of the on-boarding varies widely. Carefully matching your on-boarding plan to your director's time, availability and existing level of understanding is important. Assuming that you have recruited a very talented board, getting their best advice will depend on their detailed understanding of your company issues, challenges and opportunities.

19. Narrow list of potential directors and prioritize.

Now that you have some visibility into who might be willing to join your board, make your final list in order of your preferences. Eliminate some candidates if they do not meet your expectations.

20. Conduct face-to-face interviews including all selection committee members: educate candidates on company and determine their level of interest.
Contact each candidate and arrange interviews with key interviewers. These interviews can be one-on-one or with two interviewers. I discourage three. From my experience, it simply gets too confusing for the interviewee to give meaningful responses to the demands of three people in one session that usually lasts only one and one half to two hours - frequently over lunch or dinner.

Give the prospects some idea of what they can expect. Tell them about the company, good and bad. Gage their interest. Circle back and share each interview with the rest of the selection group. Based on these first impressions determine who you want to have other interviewers meet. Arrange and conduct interviews for all viable candidates by all key decision makers if possible.

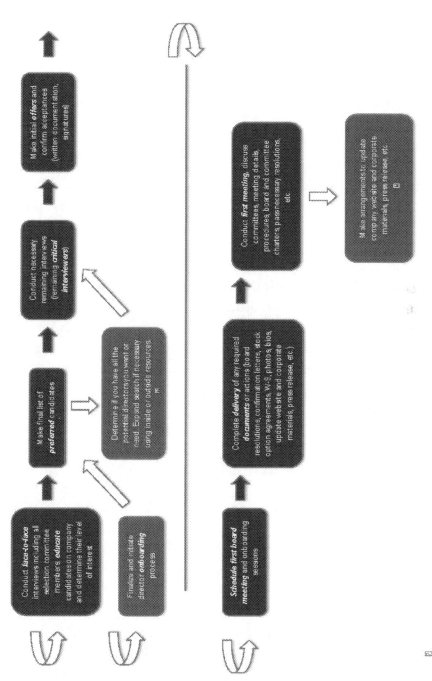

Conduct *face-to-face* interviews including all selection committee members *educate* candidates on company and determine their level of interest

Finalize and initiate director *onboarding* process

Make final list of *preferred* candidates

Determine if you have all the potential directors you want or need. Expand search if necessary using inside or outside resources

Conduct necessary remaining interviews (remaining *critical interviewers*)

Make initial *offers* and confirm acceptances (written documentation, signatures)

Schedule first board meeting and onboarding sessions

Complete *delivery* of any required *documents* or actions (board resolutions, confirmation letters, stock option agreements, W-9, photos, bios, update website and corporate materials, press release, etc.)

Conduct *first meeting*: discuss committees, meeting details, procedures, board and committee charter, pass necessary resolutions, etc.

Make arrangements to update company website and corporate materials, press release, etc.

21. Make final list of preferred candidates.

List out your final wish list of potential board members. You can list as many as you want - more than you might need or want, if you like. You will not actually end up inviting them all to join.

22. Determine if you have all the potential directors you want or need. Expand search if necessary using inside or outside resources.

Have you satisfactorily met all the requirements of your skills/experience matrix? Are you missing anything important? Are you excited about the prospects of working with any and all of the candidates? You should be. If you are not, then it might be time to reconsider you candidate.

23. Conduct necessary remaining interviews. Make certain to include all remaining critical interviewers.

Complete the interviewing process. Make certain that you have received input from all the necessary stakeholders. If your culture is such that family socializing is important, particularly including the director's spouse, then include the necessary interviews (or just an appropriate social get-together).

24. Make initial offers to the preferred candidates.

The offer letter should include the key details of time expectations, term (if any) and compensation. Insure that a signed letter is returned confirming acceptance.

With the list and interviews done, it's time for 'the ask'. Depending on the tone and details of your process to date, this might be a phone call, or a dinner, or anything in between. It's good practice to have an offer letter prepared. Your primary executive or owner would sign it and it would list the key details of the directorship. The candidate would accept by signing two copies and returning one to you.

25. Finalize onboarding plan and initiate director on-boarding process.

Complete your plan, document it and distribute it to all the necessary personnel.

26. Schedule the first board meeting and the necessary onboarding sessions.

Complete the delivery of any required documents or actions to the pending directors. Schedule on-boarding for your new directors - together or individually. Collectively schedule the first board meeting. Tie up any loose ends.

27. Have all necessary board resolutions, confirmation letters, stock option agreements, etc. signed by the current board. Get any required documents from pending directors including W-9, photos, bios, etc.

This is a step where many boards fail. The management drags its feet and procrastinates in putting all the documents and details in place. If there are any necessary resolutions, have them ready. If there is a stock option plan, then have the agreements for the directors prepared. If you require consulting, NDA or confidentiality agreements of the directors, have them ready to go. Get the copies of their identity documents that you need, along with completed W-9, photos, bios, etc. Be professional and get your new relationship with your directors off to a good start. Then, of course, prepare your agenda and presentation(s) for the first meeting.

28. Conduct the first board meeting.

This speaks for itself. Don't look here for any details on conducting the meeting however.

29. Make arrangements to update company website and corporate materials, press release, etc.

Take quick advantage of your new asset. There are many facets to having a fiduciary board. One important one is the public perception of best-of-class governance that comes with an impressive board.

Move quickly to update company materials, online and offline, to reflect the details of the board.

In Summary

This chapter presents a very simplified sequence of steps to create a board of directors. It is just one version; mine, although it has been thoroughly vetted over about five decades. You will find this progression to be a workable approach to implementing a fiduciary board, and in general, an advisory board as well.

Over the last few years, a catch phrase has become popular in board circles – 'the new normal'. This refers to the increasing interest and effort directed toward a higher standard of good governance in terms of best practices and compliance. This is particularly true among public enterprises – driven by regulatory requirements and shareholder activism. But it also applies to private enterprises – driven by aspirations and meaningful value addition.

Chapter 6

A Primer: The Ins and Outs of Board Meetings

In any company, most of the activities and functions of a board of directors are focused on, and conducted in, 'the board meeting.' The tone and content of this meeting is critical to the level of governance and ultimate value of having a board. Yet outside of the board's inner circle, few people know what typically goes on in one, much less how to organize and effectively conduct one.

What is in This Chapter?

What does a board do? They have meetings. This chapter will tell you about the purpose, frequency, agenda and structure of these meetings. It will also cover things like committees, voting and executive sessions.

The board meeting. I doubt that there could be any specific company function and venue that are as synonymous as *the board of directors* and *the board meeting*. In fact, in terms of the general awareness of most employees (and even most executives and shareholders), you would be hard pressed to find any that could name something a director actually does beyond attend the *board meetings*. In addition, unless you have attended a board meeting as a member, guest or presenter, it may be hard to imagine what actually goes on in one.

Many people will advise that managing your board is about individually managing your directors. Certainly it is critical that you have individual interaction with each one, and pursue the opportunity to impart your issues to them, unfettered by general board discussion. It is also very important to be able to listen to their individual input without others listening in. However, in managing your board, center stage is the *meeting* itself.

The board meeting is the primary way that boards function, and the dynamics between the directors, and between directors and management, is crucial. The information here is intended to help make your board meetings effective, productive, and valuable for everyone involved - especially management, directors and the shareholders (owners) who selected the board.

Meeting Frequency

One of the first questions asked about a board - right after "Who is on it?" - is how often does it meet. A board cannot be effective if it doesn't get together regularly. Some boards meet monthly, especially early-stage or fast growing companies where a lot can change in a short time. I like this approach when the company is young and there are frequent shifts in the business and the marketplace, and the company's execution is not really perfected yet. A comparable scenario is when perhaps the firm has been stable but now the market or competitive landscape is rapidly changing for some reason. In this situation one approach that works well is a board meeting in person once per quarter, with the other two meetings that quarter by teleconference.

However, for many mature private companies, a monthly board meeting can be overkill. One alternative is twice a quarter. The idea is to have one meeting mid quarter and one meeting after the quarter has been completed. This works well for a public company, when the board needs to review the quarterly numbers before they are reported to the public.

I think eight meetings a year is a great heartbeat for a board and this schedule works well for all kinds of companies. Some boards only meet once a quarter. I generally encourage those boards to meet over the phone for an update in between the face-to-face meetings. Those update calls/meetings are less formal than a full board meeting, but they keep the board engaged in the business and connecting with each other.

Authors Note:

In May 2013 I had the honor of being a keynote presenter at the Private Company Governance Summit in Washington, D.C. There were about thirty speakers in total. Someone asked me what I thought of the information presented by the others. I said that in my opinion no one said anything wrong. It made me realize that I believe, (a) there are usually several right answers and approaches in any situation, but (b) there are definitely many wrong ones as well. The information in this book is what I have found works over my fifty years of serving on corporate boards of directors.

It is important to determine the board meeting schedule a year in advance. This helps everyone plan their time to insure their availability. Of course there will always be cases when a last minute meeting is needed to discuss or approve some time sensitive issue.

Meeting Structure

Board meetings can last anywhere from a few minutes to many hours. Typically, they should last between two to four hours. Depending on how current everyone is and the magnitude of issues up for discussion, more time may be necessary. However, more than three hours of intense discussion will typically be overkill. You should always schedule a little more time than you feel will be needed. It is far better to end early than to have to rush the discussion, short-change another topic, or overrun everyone's schedule. Whether the chairperson or the CEO runs the meetings, it is much better when they are kept on schedule and on topic.

Board meetings should be discussions. They should be interactive. There should certainly be some structure, but in my experience they begin to lose their value if they are too rigid. Don't let your board be just a formality or a *rubber stamp*. Some CEOs and chairpersons make the mistake of driving the board line-by-line through the agenda, cutting off meaty discussions in the name of staying on schedule. The purpose of board meetings is not only to inform and educate your advisors, but to seek their views and advice, which requires that they be given sufficient time to talk and discuss. Getting through the agenda on time should only be a secondary goal. Board meetings should contain a large interactive component.

There are a few techniques that I've observed over the years that I like a lot. The first is the board *deck*, the pre-prepared management presentation, usually a PowerPoint, normally sent out at least three or four days in advance. The deck should include all the important financial and operational information and key performance indicators (KPIs) for the board to review in advance. These often take the form of a 'dashboard' that the board has helped shape over time into an effective tool for keeping the performance pulse of the enterprise.

It should also tee up any big discussion items selected or required for that meeting, so that the board can start to think about them in advance. Depending on each company's situation, condition and tradition, it may not be necessary for the board to go through a line-by-line review of the financial and operational results in the meeting. The CEO or chairman can ask the board members if there are any questions on the numbers, and time should be set aside in the event that a consensus of members would like to have a discussion of the operating results.

The second technique I like a lot is when the CEO puts out a list in advance of the three or four things that are 'keeping me up at night'. This can be a way of teeing up the discussion items for the meeting, or it can just be a good way for the board to quickly get an insight into the CEO's state-of-mind. One approach to this is using the 'keeping me up at night' slide to show the items that were on the slide the prior meeting and the items that are on the list currently. This shows issues that have been 'resolved' in the time since the last meeting, those things that have not been resolved, and the new things that have popped up.

Most meetings I have participated in made some attempt to follow *Robert's Rules of Order*, however it is always a very light touch, and I have yet to encounter an expert. This is definitely a case of the personal preference of the chairperson. Having no rules of engagement is a formula for pandemonium; and too much rigidity can be both time-consuming and tedious.

Meeting Agenda

There are certain traditional agenda categories. These include:

- *Approval of minutes.*
- *CEO's review/overview of the preceding period.*
- *Operation report.*
- *Finance.*
- *Sales.*
- *Marketing.*
- *Compensation.*
- *Committee reports.*
- *Technology/product discussion.*
- *Strategy/special items.*
- *Resolutions.*
- *Old/new business.*

There can also be a less functionally related, more issue related, perspective. This might include numbers, customers, people, product(s), capital, market place, competition, etc. Over time a board will refine its own approach to its agenda. Consistency is important in that it lends itself to better tracking and milestone alignment.

One of the principal work products of a board meeting is minutes. There are many acceptable formats. Very few directors, or even attorneys, get hung up on this. The most frequent difference of opinion comes on content – more or less? Minutes may become *discoverable* should the company ever be engaged in litigation. In a very closely held firm this may not be an issue, but in a more widely held, or public entity, this is an important consideration. It is generally considered to be best practice to include enough detail in the body of the minutes to document that certain topics were considered and discussed. However, it is not generally advisable to include too many specifics or details, as this could potentially compromise confidential information should the minutes become public.

Another consideration that gets varied opinions is which non-board members should be invited to the meeting as guests. There are of course certain infrequent meetings when it is not appropriate to have any guests, save corporate counsel. There are also usually certain segments of each meeting that should be limited to directors only. Then there is an executive session when even non-independent directors (management) should be excluded. There is more on this topic later.

I consider it good practice to expose a wide range of company executives to the board. Having several different managers present to the board on their specific areas of responsibility over the course of the year best does this. In addition, discussion can be scheduled of a particular subject or business area, and several executives can be present for the discussion and board questions. I see tremendous value in this. The employees get exposed to your board. This sends a strong message of professionalism and openness to outside ideas. It supports a positive culture. They of course also get direct feedback from your knowledgeable directors. For the directors' benefit they get on-going exposure to your best and brightest. This gives them insight into potential roles for these folks and aids in succession planning at all levels of your organization.

Executive Session

One of the most important techniques I've observed over the years is the executive session of the board, usually at the end of the meeting. This is when the Board meets without the CEO and other management board members or guests in the room. This allows for a discussion of the meeting.

If this is done consistently it simply offers a more open forum for the independent directors to talk freely, and when or if there actually is a delicate issue, the session can be conducted without unnecessarily alarming anyone. The executive session can be five minutes or it can be a half hour. Sometimes there is very little to discuss; sometimes there is a lot. The CEO should be briefed on the executive session; either by the board afterwards, or by the Chairman or lead director shortly after the meeting ends. This is an opportunity for the board to provide feedback to the CEO on the business, the team, his own performance, and the strategy. Boards should not miss this opportunity to provide feedback and in a healthy relationship the CEO should demand it of them.

Committees

The board of a public company requires certain committees. The private company fiduciary board does not. However, if the goal is to replicate standard governance there are typically committees.

Committees are used to reduce the amount of time necessary for the board to address detailed matters. The objective is to have board members on a committee for which they have more in-depth expertise than perhaps other directors. The committee is used to pre-review its designated matters and make an informed recommendation to the full board. This does not diminish the board's responsibilities, but does serve to streamline business.

The first committee is always audit/finance. Without getting into any detail here, it oversees finance, most importantly accounting in general and audits in particular. Usually second is compensation, which monitors and pre-approves all compensation issues involving executives, board members and other relevant employees and important considerations. Generally, the committee sets certain standard parameters to be approved by the board, and themselves pre-approve specific situations as their charter sets forth. Recently a newer committee has emerged: governance. Its oversight may include regulatory matters, succession, recruiting of employees and directors, and board policies and procedures in general.

Additional committees may include strategy, technology, M&A, and others deemed key to the company's success and the boards' responsibilities.

Phone Meetings and Special Meetings

Governing documents for most entities provide that board meetings may be conducted by teleconference rather than in person. Face-to-face has many advantages, of course, but short notice and convenience may not always be two of them.

Regularly scheduled meetings that are held via telephone should be conducted through a teleconference bridge, and may go through the normal graphic presentation, like a PowerPoint that was delivered in advance. They may also utilize a web-based audio/video collaboration connection tool like GoToMeeting (©Citrix Online).

It is helpful to keep these meetings somewhat shorter than regular ones, and more effort needs to be made by the chairperson to mediate between the parties wishing to speak. Care should always be taken to ask if anyone else has comments before moving on to the next subject. Some directors, like me, tend to say less during phone meetings, showing the restraint to avoid saying something that has already been adequately articulated by another director.

Special or unscheduled meetings may be held at any time, in-person or by phone. The board should have an effective method of notifying everyone in accordance with the company's governing documents, and everyone should properly RSVP. Such meetings require the same procedures and minutes as any other meeting.

They Hate Me

Leonard was a seasoned CEO, but he had a strong inclination to want to please everyone. One afternoon we were leaving a board meeting that had been held in the offices of one of the leading Silicon Valley law firms. Len walked out with a frown and promptly kicked the tire of his rental car hard stating, "They hate me!" I said, "What are you talking about?" He said, "That last vote proves that those VC directors all hate me." Trying to understand I said, "Len, you won on that issue, the vote was five to four." He quickly responded, "Well, those four still hate me"

Voting

Arguably the most tangible product of a board meeting is a vote. It takes some amount of experience, and often advice of counsel, to discern what requires a vote, and what may work better as simply guidance. Voting probably represents the board's strictest adherence to Robert's Rules of Order. Items up for a vote require a formal resolution. It is very important to have a clear statement of the resolution, agreed upon by the board, stated in the minutes.

The most common misconception I encounter regarding voting is that all votes must be unanimous. Why? I have no idea where this concept originated, but it is of course generally false. Only written consent must be unanimous. There are certain votes, stipulated by the company's governing documents, which may require a 'super majority' (more than 51%, e.g. 66.67%), like an acquisition or financing transaction. There may also be a specific term of a class of preferred stock that requires the vote of a director representing that class. However, only these special cases require anything more than a simple majority. There will certainly be things that everyone agrees on, but constructive dissent is healthy. Sometimes, when everyone has properly reviewed an issue previously, but no vote was taken (perhaps being postponed to await additional information), it may be efficient to get a board vote without a meeting. This is called Written Consent, or Unanimous Written Consent. This procedure allows the distribution of the resolution via email, FAX, or letter, with the board members responding with their vote in kind.

When in doubt, go ahead and conduct a vote. Keep in mind that the definitive nature of a vote serves both to give management clear direction, and to demonstrate to outsiders that the board faithfully fulfilled its fiduciary responsibilities to review and rule on key issues.

In Summary

Board meetings should not be operational reporting sessions with information flowing one way. They should not be solely for the benefit of the board. They should be for the benefit of the CEO, the senior team, and ultimately the owners. A productive board meeting should be an appropriate (to each unique company culture) combination of formality and informality. There should be an adequate agenda, process, frequency, and length. There should be meaningful discussion of important topics and minimal discussion of minor ones. Voting should be respectful and definitive. There should be an appropriate use and recognition of other elements like committees and executive sessions.

I've always loved the idea of a 'kitchen cabinet' and to me that is what a great board meeting should feel like. The best boards act as a team of experienced, skilled, engaged, and helpful advisors and meetings should be a place and a time for that group to provide the most help and assistance they can. It is the CEO and chairperson's job to make sure that happens, and on a regular basis.

Chapter 7

Company to Director, You're Fired!

Most seasoned CEOs, chairmen or private company owners don't hesitate to fire an employee that simply does not fit; yet they can be hesitant and indecisive when it comes to asking a director to step down. Making such a move is fraught with sensitive considerations, and requires great finesse.

What is in This Chapter?

Hiring a director is one thing. Getting one to leave gracefully is another. This chapter discusses why and when you should fire a director. It covers differences between public and private companies, and recommends approaches to this termination. It also includes some war stories.

How do you fire a director? If you have been a fan of Donald Trump's TV show *The Apprentice*, you know that you just have to say, "you're fired!" While that might be just fine for The Donald, and for firing an employee, for some reason, firing a board member can often be much more intimidating. Perhaps this is because, unlike a subordinate, many directors are often more senior and successful in their career than the company CEO. They are likely to be highly respected leaders in their field, which may be why they were invited to join the board in the first place. Regardless, all directors serve at the pleasure of the owners of the company, whether that means public shareholders, private owners, family members, private equity group, or one individual.

These days for any company there are a multitude of Federal, and state-by-state laws and regulations as to why you may or may not terminate an employee. Issues must be carefully documented in order to ensure that you are in compliance with a myriad of rules governing employment. With directors however, to the best of my knowledge, there are no laws regarding their termination. The only exception would be any terms of service within the corporate articles, such as a 'morals clause'.

Directors are rarely employees, but rather typically they are the elected representatives of the voting shareholders in the firm. As such, no justification, reason, or transgression is required to justify termination. It may be with or without cause, which really only affects severance issues that may be part of the corporate charter. The shareholders (read owners) may terminate a director's service at will, only based on the timing stipulated in the company charter or articles of incorporation, with proper notifications, board and shareholder votes, and required regulatory filings.

The termination vote would usually be at a regularly scheduled, or specially called, shareholders meeting. In a private or closely held company, this can be called most any time by the majority ownership. The board can recommend this, or controlling shareholders can demand this based on the company's terms of incorporation. No reason for termination need be given, although of course one usually is.

Private Versus Public

The differences between private and public board terminations are primarily in matters of the details of incorporation, including the state regulations, those associated with the SEC and listing exchanges (if public), and of course the increased sensitivity to public relations due to the effect of material events on the stock. Under all circumstances, whether the company is private or public, corporate counsel should provide appropriate advice in advance of any actions.

In a privately owned firm, the process may be simpler, although the board should still at least discuss the above considerations. In this case, the initial discussions about terminating a board member can be initiated by a director, senior executive, or, in fact, any shareholder.

The more closely held the ownership, the less complicated the process of gaining appropriate consensus. When determining a course of action, the person initiating the movement to terminate a director should consider the composition and personalities of the board. If there were a clearly dominant shareholder then I would recommend approaching them first with concerns. If there were a clearly dominate personality on the board - chairman or not - I would recommend them as the next logical choice. It is more complicated if the director in question is the/a founder, or substantial shareholder, or plays an active and important role in managing the company. This requires somewhat more finesse.

This is usually encountered in a company that has obtained institutional capital, most likely venture capital. In this situation, it is not uncommon for the investors to have acquired voting control through one or more preferred funding rounds. When these investors feel that it is not in the best interest of the company for the founder to continue in their current role, they may seek to oust them completely from the company. It is typical for the founder's role to be diminished over time, with their board seat being the last step. If the investors continue to see their participation as disruptive or divisive, they will attempt to eliminate their directorship as well.

It is preferable to try reason and negotiation in arriving at the terms of departure, doing it honorably and professionally. This of course assumes that both parties put the value of the enterprise above their own personal agendas – e.g., exercising their fiduciary responsibilities. However, these actions can turn emotional and contentious quickly. At that point only voting control and existing corporate documentation prevail.

Shoot Straight

Since firing a director can easily end in recrimination and even lawsuits, I recommend great care be taken. The following actions may achieve a satisfactory resolution:

- *Have a candid discussion with the individual, explaining the issues and how the decision maker(s) feel about them, noting perhaps "Why would you want to stay on the board under the circumstances."*
- *Coax them to resign - for the sake of their reputation and the best interests of the organization.*
- *Be prepared to offer some incentives to ease the move, like some accelerated vesting on unvested stock options or the continuation of some benefits (if they are currently receiving any)… or even just a favorable press release.*

Agree to a mutual release and confidentiality agreement.

If the timing permits, you may want to ask for their resignation as part of a broader adjustment/announcement such as a new financing, new investor, 'upgrading' the board with a new member, reducing board size, or other reasonable trigger.

Director Firings: War stories

Sometimes the firing of a director can be sad, humorous, and strange, all at the same time. Here are several such cases that I have been involved in.

You're Out...Oops, Maybe Not: In the mid '90s I was on the board of a private Internet company. There were seven directors - the founder/CEO (who directly and indirectly voted a majority of the stock), a friend of mine, who was chairman and had recruited me; a high-level tech exec who represented his company as a strategic investor; three other stellar execs that I personally knew and recruited to join this board; and me.

One day in the midst of a regularly scheduled board meeting, with no warning, the CEO asked three of us, including the chairman to resign. He simply said that he did not want us on the board anymore. We knew that it was a result of a difference of opinion on certain strategic issues – including when to target an IPO. Having majority control he called the shots.

The remaining three directors had no choice, however the strategic investor informed the CEO that the remaining board would not support him as chairman, and none of the other three were willing to assume the role. This created a snag. Therefore, the founder must retain one of the three of us deposed directors as chairman. He then asked the three of us to step out of the room while the board discussed the chairmanship.

When we were invited back to the meeting the CEO had selected the colleague that I had recruited (who had actually previously been CEO of one of the fastest companies to ever go from zero to public on the NYSE). The new chairman promptly then quipped, "This is the strangest board meeting I have ever been in. One minute I'm being fired, and the next I'm the darn chairman."

A Founder's Dilemma: I was once on the board of a healthcare technology company that I had originally conceptualized and was the seed investor. I even recruited the founder to leave the company he previously founded, which was then public. (He was no longer its CEO.)

Things progressed well with him as the CEO of this new firm. We soon raised venture capital, and the CEO was pressured by the new investors to add a director of their choice. All of the other outside directors had seats tied to their investment; I did not. Also on the board was a nominal co-founder. As the VP engineering he was a terrific technology manager but a poor director. He never spoke a word outside of his specific presentation on the progress of the product.

Given that a new class of preferred institutional investors were making a move to consolidate their control of the board, and given that in the future good governance would dictate eliminating the VP from the board anyway (as a second employee inside director), the best governance decision would have been to keep me (his chosen outside director) and remove the VP, but he did not. He chose to keep the weaker and vulnerable director, and keep 'harmony' with his investors, which can come back to haunt a CEO sometimes.

He 'fired' me by simply saying that he wanted me to resign. He gave me the reason, but there was little discussion. He kept me on the advisory board for a while and continued some vesting of options.

A Tale of Two Founders: Entrepreneurs, who succeed in starting companies, and securing outside investors, often face a challenge when their firm grows and, in the investors' opinion, the founder's skills are no longer up to the requirements of their current position. This scenario is often profiled in the business press. Here are two such tales.

Lance founded his firm with a partner. He was the business brain and his partner was the technical talent. The company had about nine different rounds of venture capital investment. There were almost twenty different VCs involved. The board of nine was Lance, seven VCs, and me.

Over the course of about ten years the board fired Lance as CEO three times. Each time he reverted to chairman of the board. A replacement CEO was brought in. Lance still worked hard and constructively on business development and strategic alliances. Twice, the new CEOs did not work out, and twice Lance was brought back as CEO. Lance stepped up. The third time the replacement CEO succeeded in taking the company public and all were rewarded accordingly.

Sal founded his firm alone. He recruited a good team, developed their product, and got traction with some customers. The company then attracted term sheets from two pairs of VCs. He selected the pair that I felt would be the less forgiving under pressure. He found out what that meant. Things were not going well at one point. The board 'promoted' Sal to chairman and relieved him of his CEO duties. He remained active in a business development role, however his actions proved very disruptive to operations and he did not cooperate well with the new CEO. He frequently interfered with both sales and operations employees. After being reprimanded a few times, the board had no choice but to terminate him completely. The company was ultimately sold, but failed to return anything to shareholders.

I May Ask You to Resign: With a small, private or early-stage company, when it starts to grow or mature, it is often advisable to 'upgrade' a director to someone with more experience or stature. This is a common occurrence.

I recently recruited a C-level executive from a $14 billion technology company to join the board of a small but profitable software development firm. In the process the executive said to me, "Our company policy will only allow me to sit on one outside board. Why should it be yours?"

After a moment's pause my response was, "Do you have any other offers?"

"No."

"If you join ours now, you can always resign if something else comes along. In the meantime, we can work together and learn from each other. But...if I ever have the chance to get your CEO on this board, I will be asking you to resign." He joined and continues to be a tremendous asset.

In Summary

Over time things change. Over time the needs of any company change. There may come a time when the company needs to add additional skill sets or experience. There are also times when the behavior of a single board member may be an obstacle to the board's best performance. In my experience being involved at the board level with an interesting company can be rewarding and educational. However, it is always worth remembering that a board director is not a lifetime position. Be prepared to roll with the circumstances. This may mean that sometimes you may be the automobile's windshield – the one needing to diplomatically ease another director out, or sometimes you may be the bug – the one being unceremoniously ousted. Good advice to everyone involved is to keep your professionalism and sense of humor.

Chapter 8

Private Company Profiles: One Size Does Not Fit All

Private companies - this is such a broad category. When looking at their origin, their growth process, and their hoped-for 'end-game', there are actually many varieties – just like flowers. There are many different looks, different sizes, different shapes, and certainly different smells. These differences play a big part in determining which format for a board of directors would be the most effective and create the most value for a company's ownership.

What is in This Chapter?

While public companies are publically owned, private firms have a wide variety of differences. This chapter describes those differences and gives insights into how those variations and the stage of development of the company affect the characteristics of their boards. It also, explains why the formation of a board does not mean loosing absolute control of your own company.

One can find a great deal of information on how private companies differ from public ones. Much of this information is about the legal details, but some addresses the motivations and management. However, there is little if any information on how private companies might differ from each other. As is almost always the case, even the writing on this tends to focus on only the large cap companies. I have seen almost nothing exploring the details and issues of smaller private firms. Here we seek to explain these differences: those between small and mid-size business entities, across several criteria, and how those differences effect the functioning of a fiduciary board of directors.

Let's start with the similarities. The most simplistic definition of a private company is that it is not public. That is to say, it is not listed on any trading exchange or stock market, it is not listed in or on any regulated over-the-counter market, and it does not have more than the maximum number of shareholders that require additional filings with agencies such as the SEC (Securities and Exchange Commission) and FINRA (Financial Industry Regulatory Authority).

The U.S. Securities Exchange Act of 1934, section 12(g), generally limits a privately held company to fewer than 500 shareholders. One of the reasons for this may be that the SEC considers 500 shareholders to actually be quasi-public, and for shareholder protection should be required to provide the same shareholder information and disclosures as a public entity.

The JOBS (Jumpstart Our Business Startups) Act, which became law in April 2012, raises the maximum number of shareholders a company can have before it's required to register with the SEC from 500 to 2,000. While technically private, companies in this category still must adhere to governance principles that base their fiduciary responsibilities on the rights of those smaller minority shareholders anyway.

With this in mind, let's continue to narrow our definition down further. For the purposes of a board of directors I would exclude any type of business whose sole purpose is to provide a basic income to a single owner or family – *basic* here arbitrarily meaning under $1,000,000 per year. This includes your corner bakery, a sole or small practitioner professional (consultant, doctor, lawyer, etc.), most single-location businesses, such as a retail store.

We do however want to <u>include</u> start-ups, and early-stage companies whose plan and goal is to grow much larger than the aforementioned ones – regardless of whether they were financed by founders, venture capital funds, angels or others. This leaves us with any company having fewer than 500 shareholders, un-registered securities, and intending to provide enterprise value beyond (hopefully far beyond) basic income for one family.

We can further differentiate these private companies from each other in four categories:

1. *Number of shareholders.*
2. *Controlling interest.*
3. *Stage of development.*
4. *Management structure.*

The different combinations of characteristics from each of these groups will suggest differing approaches to a board of directors.

How Many Shareholders Are There (and Who Are They)?

Since a fiduciary board's *fiduciary* responsibility is to the shareholders or owners of the company, how many there are and who they are dictate certain policies, procedures and concerns. Starting with numbers, I will arbitrarily divide the categories up as follows:

- *One to six mostly unrelated individuals,*
- *An extended family (related individuals),*
- *Six to 50 unrelated parties,*
- *Over 50 individual shareholders.*

If another company owns the private company, then I would typically look to the ownership of that firm.

Although the 'who', and more importantly 'who has control', are two separate questions, each type of owner normally exercises their control in different ways. Ultimately, how owners exert their control of a private company has a dramatic effect on selecting a board style, the board's decision-making process, the directors themselves, and ultimately their authority and responsibilities.

Are the shareholders mostly employees or mostly non-employees? A family? Are the outside investors angels, a venture capital firm or firms (VC), private equity investors (financial investor), or strategic investors (e.g. another company)?

Equity Control – Controlling Interest

When looking at equity or voting control - legal majority ownership control, it is worthwhile to differentiate between dominant control (e.g. usually over 66%) and barely controlling interest (e.g. just over 50%). It is also worth understanding whether one must combine several like-minded owners to achieve either of these levels, or can one person vote the entire stake. Variations in the combination of ownership constituting control will often lead to nuances in the way a well-designed and well-led board will deal with various types of issues.

One important and little acknowledged subtlety has two opposing perspectives. In my experience, many company leaders, who do not themselves have equity control, are uncomfortable when a board vote is anything less than unanimous. Regardless of the governance reality that the majority prevails, they feel that they have failed in some way if anyone disagrees. On the other hand, an exceptionally close vote on an issue can put the validity of the decision in question.

Keep in mind that each director likely has skills and experience that differ to one degree or another from their colleagues. Yet they all get the same single vote. What if the directors that might be deemed to be more knowledgeable on the topic in question vote in the minority? It can lead one to question the wisdom of the majority decision. There are very few absolutes in board deliberations and decisions. Most activities are very subjective – relying on the knowledge and judgment of the directors. Once, after delivering a keynote address at a conference on private company governance, I was asked what I thought of the presentations by the other thirty-five speakers at the event. My immediate response was positive. I said that I was impressed, and did not actually hear anyone say anything wrong. When asked what I meant by that I commented that there were some statements made, and concepts presented, that I did not agree with but they were not *wrong*. There can be multiple *right* answers and approaches.

> **Definition:** *board, as favored by a venture capital investor: a group of persons having managerial, supervisory, or investigatory powers <~of directors>, comprised of one founder and a minimum of two investors.*
> *- **From an experienced entrepreneur***

Boards are like a chemistry experiment - you mix some different chemicals in different amounts to arrive at some useful solution. It is the same with public and private boards, however private boards start with a somewhat different chemical base.

I would summarize these thoughts by noting that in a private company the control that the majority ownership exerts, effects the balance the board can strike between advising and governing.

In the extreme, in a company owned by one-person, the board is elected, and can be fundamentally terminated, by that person at will. This in practice makes it an advisory board, even if it was legally formed as a fiduciary board.

In a venture capital controlled company there is usually some agreement on board composition that was part of the terms of the investment – perhaps even changing over subsequent investment rounds. The VC(s) will usually appoint a certain number of directors and agree to a certain number from management and other owners, or even some independent directors. The balance of power is dictated by these dynamics and legal agreements.

A majority of one

Many years ago I sat on a nine-member board as the sole independent director. In addition to the company founder/CEO/ chairman there were seven directors each representing a different investor. The CEO did not like non-unanimous votes. He always sought to compromise and get everyone to come to agreement. Even when voting with the majority (to make it unanimous) was not in the founder's best interest he would often do so to make it unanimous. Well, there were times I could not do that. Even though he voted with the majority I considered the issue so important that I could not do so. I can recall at least twice during the twelve years I served on that board, when we were completely stalemated at 8-1. I was always the one. But I would not change my vote. On these two occasions the CEO would not call for a final vote. He kept the discussion going, and I kept arguing my points. Both times, hours later when we voted, it was unanimous - I had successfully convinced everyone else to vote with me.

Company Stage of Development

Adding further to the matrix of board considerations is the stage of development the company is in. This can sometimes equate to age, but not necessarily.

- *Is the company a start-up, with no revenue?*
- *Is it operating, generating revenue, and approaching cash flow neutral – regardless of age?*
- *Is it cash flow positive?*

In the last example age does enter into the equation. A young company that is profitable is different than an old one that may have struggled previously and is now profitable, or one that has been profitable for a longer period of time. Is the company likely to experience fast or slow growth going forward? Is the company being positioned for long-term ownership, or being groomed for sale or an IPO (initial public offering)?

Management

The next consideration, which impacts the board dynamics, is management. Specifically, who is the most senior manager – chief executive officer, president, principal, managing director, executive director, or manager? Is this individual the founder, a founder, a non-owner promoted from within the company, or a professional manager recruited from outside the company? How experienced are they? Have they run an independent company of the same or larger size? Have they reported to, or managed a board of directors?

All of this detail is like spices in a stew – or elements in a chemistry experiment.

Pulling it Together

So far we have explored a number of variables - how many shareholders and who they are, who has controlling interest, the stage of development, and the management of a private company. These are set against the foundational framework of the details of incorporation – sole proprietorship, partnership, Sub S (Sub Chapter S IRS designation),

LLC (limited liability corporation), or C (traditional) corporation. All these elements combine to create a unique environment requiring an optimal balance of considerations in forming a board of directors.

Each of these characteristics will alter what I consider to be the key governance dynamic within any private company - the majority ownership/the executive management/the board of directors.

There are of course stakeholders in the company beyond these three. These include employees, customers, vendors, financial and strategic relationships, and perhaps others. However, as much as these constituencies are affected by the governance decisions, none

---

The dog in the boardroom

I was the chairman of a tech company. The board also included a CEO who I had recruited from the outside, two independent directors, and two venture capitalists. The company was forced to do a slightly down investment round (a new financing at a valuation below the previous round). This new round included a new venture fund.

At the start of the next board meeting after the closing, the managing partner representing the new fund on the board entered the room. He proceeded to circulate all the way around the room greeting and making comments to each person. One director turned to another and asked. "What just happened?"

The director replied, "Oh, don't mind him. As the newest investor he is just figuratively urinating in the four corners of the room and the conference table to mark his territory."

---

generally enter into these decisions. The only exception here is where there are specific contracts or agreements granting them a say so, for example as might be found in some bank lending covenants.

The Philosophy of Decision Making - Checks and Balances

As we have discussed, each detail and variation in the ownership of the company will contribute to forming its composition or 'DNA'. This profile will usually tend to lend itself to different paths through the governance process.

Keep in mind that this process is not static. It starts with the formation of the board, but winds its way through all the trials and tribulations of the company's existence - through good economic times and bad. Through missed and maximized opportunities.

The more ownership in the company any individual director, or group of directors has (founders, family, VC, PEG, strategic investor, or outside individual) the more difficult it becomes for an independent director to balance their fiduciary responsibilities. When a majority owner's best interests diverge from those of the minority shareholders', an independent director has to carefully weigh their advice and decisions and focus on 'enterprise value'. Any CEO who has managed a company through the *Zone of Insolvency* (a pre-bankruptcy period) will tell you that one of the best ways to test your actions is to be informed and act in good faith on behalf of building 'enterprise value'.

Let's look at just one of hundreds of potential situations...

A founder/CEO owns 51%. A venture capital firm, or combination of firms in a single class of stock, own the rest. The terms of the venture capital investment included two board seats on a five-person board. The founder gets two, one for themselves and one for another member of management. The investment agreement allocated one seat for an independent director, mutually agreed on. Who recruited the independent? What is his/her background? Will they understand or relate more to the viewpoint of an entrepreneur or an investor? Do the investors own common stock or preferred shares? Are there any preferred terms that require approval of the entire class of shares before any specific action can be taken, e.g. acquisition or sale?

In every different situation there is a delicate balance between management, inside ownership, outside investors and the board - including these plus any independent (*independent* by whose definition?) directors. Any preference rights with a specific class of stock (typically later round investors, rarely founder's shares) can dramatically change the decision making process regardless of board composition (the collection of board director's backgrounds and perspectives).

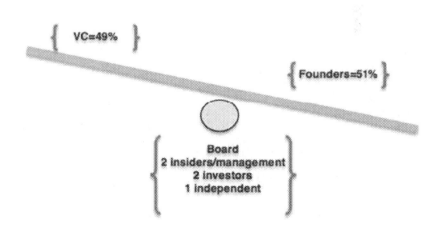

Beyond the numerical majority voting control of the board, or the underlying shareholders or unit holders themselves, there is the value of outside perspective. Does the board represent a balance of interests, viewpoints and foundational experience?

In the end, it's a numbers game. At every stage of the formation of a company, the establishment of a board, and the involvement of outside investors, there are strategic actions that can be taken which may well have significant implications in the future.

One simple example is the timing and composition of an initial board. It can be a very savvy move to form a fiduciary board early in the company's evolution rather than waiting until you get outside capital and are required to add investors to the board. There is far more leverage and benefit to founders when new outside investor directors are added to an already existing board over configuring a board initially comprised of these investor appointees. Many decisions can be made by a board in advance of investor members joining that are completely appropriate, however might not get decided or acted on in the same way when requiring post-investor approval.

In Summary

While there are a wide variety of types of private companies, they will all generally have concentrated and clearly defined ownership, it is that ownership that directly elects or appoints a board of directors. Therefore, the directors have very clear guidelines for their fiduciary duty. For a privately held company the real purpose of a board is to provide management with the broadest and deepest perspective and advice possible for them to effectively run the business. The board should also augment the skills and experience of management, assist in assessing and addressing the risks to the business, provide insights into strategic direction, and enforce checks and balances over the judgment, ethics and actions of management.

In a privately owned enterprise, the right board agenda will be a reflection of the number and nature of the owners or shareholders. Taking into consideration the best interests of controlling shareholders, but giving adequate consideration to those of minority shareholders. Even the terms 'owner' and 'shareholder' reflect differences.

Owners give the impression of an entity, closely held by a single (or very small number of) individual(s).

Shareholders (or unit holders) give the impression of an entity that has 'outsider' investors or ownership, and therefore potentially more diverse interests. This then creates a spectrum or scale of board responsibility bridging the extremes between individual and diverse ownership. This scale ranges between a maximum advisory role with a minimum fiduciary role, and a maximum fiduciary role with accompanying advisory role.

Each private enterprise should choose and balance board objectives and behaviors between these factors. The recent trends in regulatory oversight of public company governance and disclosures have created best practices standards for enterprise behavior. There is good reason for private companies - regardless of the specific *breed* - to seek to appropriately emulate these standards, including the formation of a fiduciary board of directors.

Chapter 9

4-D Diversity – When Is Board Diversity Actually Diverse?

Since a private company can put anyone the owners want on their board, with little or no public exposure or issues, why should they care about diversity? Why wouldn't they simply want to seat directors who think like them, look like them, behave like them, and manage like them. After all, that's what would best represent their interests, right? That's who would be in the best position to exercise their fiduciary responsibilities on the owner's behalf, right? Well, in a word, NO!

What is in This Chapter?

What is it the real goal of diversity? Why does it matter? This chapter talks about how to set up a matrix to map diversity, and what are the most important characteristics to have on your board. What are the four dimensions of diversity relative to the best interests of the board and enterprise value?

There are several topics that are mandatorily on the top of every board's list for discussion and action. The hottest ones right now include activist shareholders, cyber security risks, digital/social media, e-commerce, and more. However, none have been in the top ranks of that list longer than diversity.

To get what I consider to be a complete perspective on diversity it is worthwhile to start with some questions.

- *What industry is your company in?*
- *What part of the country or of the world are you considering expansion into?*
- *What management skill set(s) have you had a real problem attracting and retaining?*
- *What skills or business experience might complement the core expertise of your management team?*
- *Who are your customers?*
- *What is their demographic mix?*
- *Who are your employees?*
- *Where are they, and what are their demographics and range of skill sets?*
- *Who are your competitors?*
- *Do they generally do things the same way as you do?*
- *Do they make virtually the same products?*
- *Do they provide the same services, in the same way; or, are they somewhat different?*
- *Do you deal with consumers, government agencies; value added resellers, agents, distributors, and joint venture/strategic partners?*
- *Do you sell a product targeted at wealthy consumers, middle class, corporate clients, etc.?*
- *Do you have important issues related to intellectual property, patents, government regulatory authorities, or unions?*

The list goes on. If your definition of diversity is limited to race and gender then I submit that is very shortsighted, and missing the point and opportunity.

Accessing Expertise - a Diversity Matrix

When looking at all the above questions, have you seriously reflected on – or even developed a matrix of – these considerations. Which of these areas is your management team, combined with your board of directors, already expert in? For which of these areas do you lack sufficient direct experience and expertise to give you a competitive advantage? These are the highest priority for adding to the board.

No one person or company has all the knowledge or answers; and even if they did, things change. But, by the same token only a few companies can afford to hire all the experts they would like. Small, mid-size and especially private companies need to be more strategic and creative in accessing what incremental deeper expanded expertise and experience would provide a significant strategic advantage in their business.

One of the best and often underutilized methods to add critical best-of-class expertise to a company is with a board member. Pound for pound you cannot get more value for your compensation dollar than acquiring key human capital in the person of an additional or replacement director.

It is worthwhile to note that if you are targeting a management hire, clearly you want to weight their skills toward the job description. If you are looking for an advisor or advisory board member, then the weighting can be narrow and deep in the specific area of interest. However, if you are looking for a fiduciary board member you are selecting for a broad level of expertise across multiple boxes if possible, and an added element of seasoning-judgment-collaborative skills, and governance experience.

Four-D Diversity

I submit that the most progressive organizations are taking their definition and application of *diversity* to a new, more advanced level. Most discussions used to revolved around a traditional two-dimensional view of diversity - namely race and gender. I prefer a much more comprehensive four-dimensional view - namely professional skills, industry or domain expertise, demographic diversity, and geographic representation.

It is important to recognize that there is a commonly accepted 'new normal' in corporate governance. This concept encompasses a variety of more contemporary considerations for boards. Diversity is certainly among them, however even more important to the survival and prospering of an enterprise is recognizing and mitigating risk. The first step in the risk mitigation cycle is recognition. What better hedge could you have in this area than an expert 4-D diverse board and management team?

What's missing?

On one occasion, as a board member of a public company, I was asked to step in and take over as interim president and CEO of a recently acquired subsidiary that was doing about $20MM in revenue, but was insolvent and losing money. My job was to determine its viability and either close it down properly or stabilize it, set it on a path to profitability, and recruit a new CEO.

On my first day on the job I convened an all-hands meeting. All 225 employees were there and frankly quite anxious. Most had been there for a long time - many over ten and even fifteen years. They had been through four layoffs under the previous ownership. They had worked under eight CEOs in the last nine years. I explained what I was there to try to do and opened it up for questions. One man in the back of the room raised his hand and asked, "What qualifications will you be looking for in the new CEO you intend to hire?"

I responded, "Someone who has run a public technology company, a person who is decisive and has good leadership and people skills."

The man continued, "Aren't you going to look for someone with experience in the workplace training business?"

I asked, "Why would I do that?"

This employee answered, "Sir, that's the business we are in!"

I said, "I know that, but I am looking at 225 people who know that business very well. That doesn't seem to be what you have been missing."

Key Expertise/Director Candidates	A	B	C	D	E	F	G	H	I	J
Financial Expert		X					X			X
M&A	X	X			X	X	X	X		X
IPO	X		X		X	X		X	X	
B2C			X		X		X		X	X
Consumer Marketing		X	X				X		X	
Internet/Web Marketing	X	X	X		X		X	X	X	
Technology	X		X		X		X	X	X	
Retail Business		X		X	X		X		X	
Consumer Customer Service		X	X				X		X	X
Call Center Operations	X	X		X			X		X	X
Human Resources	X	X			X					
Regulatory Environment				X						
Board Experience	X	X			X		X	X		X
Board Leadership Expertise	X				X					X
CEO Experience	X	X	X		X	X		X	X	X
Comp Committee Experience		X					X			X
Male/Female	M	F	M	F	F	F	M	M	M	M

The matrix above is a very simple example that compares ten potential independent directors across seventeen categories expertise/diversity that have been identified to be critical to the future success of one particular firm. The directors listed are being proposed to fill multiple vacant seats.

In Summary

The primary objective of diversity is to benefit the company with the widest and deepest perspectives on the issues that are the most critical to the enterprise. In today's fast moving and exceptionally nuanced business environment, the more detailed information management has the better. To effectively accomplish this, the best technique is to map the preferred expertise and track those qualifications you have satisfied, and those that need strengthening. Keep in mind that diversity includes the traditional race and gender, but should be expanded to add professional skills, industry or domain expertise, which most boards now understand, as well as demographic diversity, and geographic representation.

Chapter 10

Welcome aboard to Your 'Youngster' on the Board

The addition of a new director always impacts (not always for the good) board dynamics, and if the new director is particularly young this adds even more to the challenge for both the freshman director and the board. This said, a smooth onboarding is eminently doable.

What is in This Chapter?

This chapter looks at how you bring new directors onboard, and how do you insure that they fit in and deliver the value you hope for – even if they are much younger than your other directors.

Many seasoned directors have noticed the fairly recent mini-trend, as chronicled in the business press, of much younger individuals being elected to big company boards (where the average age is sixty three). We are not talking here about successful corporate executives in their 40s, but rather entrepreneurs in their 20s or early 30s, often with little real business experience much less any board experience or even any meaningful tenure with a company having revenue or, dare we say, profits. One might think, why ... and then, OK, how can we prepare them for this responsibility?

After having had the privilege of sitting on many boards over many years, I have seen and served with the widest possible variety of directors: from ages eighteen to eighty five, from no high school diploma to multiple Ph.Ds., both genders, many ethnic backgrounds, and from zero business experience to sitting directors of Fortune 100 companies. In addition, as with most directors with at least a couple of years of service, I have also seen a full range of personalities and behaviors: nasty, disagreeably argumentative, not so bright, and even criminal, as well as delightful, polite, thoughtful, intelligent, and even lovable. While a much younger director might still represent a cross section of all the above, they may also add a distinct generational element to the equation.

This is an important time in corporate governance to ask, and try to answer, the question, "What advice would you have for these young directors so that they can blend in, be effective, and avoid making naïve youthful mistakes?" This is my attempt to do this dual objective justice.

Dynamics

From my experience, and that of many fellow directors who have shared their opinions with me, the most common single problem underlying poorly performing boards is *board dynamics;* the interpersonal relationships and communication culture within the board. A young first-time freshman director and all their welcoming (all too often upper class male) colleagues on the board, are advised to be keenly conscious of this factor. Everyone should be very comfortable with the diversity of personalities, as well as qualifications.

An old youngster

In the context of a board, not all youngsters are necessarily young. A new board member could just as easily be much older, even someone in their 50s or 60s. Many seasoned C-level executives, and professionals, such as retiring partners from large audit firms, have been discouraged or not permitted to join for-profit fiduciary boards. First-time directors also come from long careers in academia, military, government, or nonprofit sectors, and of course private or family companies.

Although they may have attended 'board meetings', or been on nonprofit boards, they still may lack some degree of familiarity with governance concepts — e.g., fiduciary responsibilities, discussion protocols, personal and corporate liabilities, committees, risk, 'nose in, fingers out' oversight, and more.

When considering the addition of a new director, it is important to weigh what skills and perspectives are needed most, along with the true need for, and value of, a uniquely young perspective. Also, if your board is adding one of these older freshman directors, it is still worth considering what governance education and company information and cultural acclimation they might need — right alongside their young colleagues.

Throughout your interview process make good use of personal interviews, and in the final stage even possibly invite the candidate to a guest sit-in on appropriate segments of a board meeting. Whether you are the 'joiner' or the 'joined,' this could avoid tremendous potential unpleasantness down the road.

This is not totally about age; however, as everyone will recognize, a potential forty to fifty year difference in age can alone be its own barrier to communicating and add stress to the passionate discussion of critical topics. All directors should agree in advance to be willing to courteously collaborate within even the tensest situations.

Regardless of the age issue, when younger individuals are being sought, there is likely to be one or more specific domains of knowledge that the board is seeking to augment. (Note: also see Chapter 9 on diversity.) I have never heard of a case where being twenty-five or thirty years old was the candidate's *sole* qualification. I believe that the reason for the youth movement is the quest for acknowledged and extraordinary expertise in specific fields such as Internet technology, social media, mobile applications, 'big data', or cybersecurity. While there are certainly older folks with these qualifications, youth is often assumed to be more current and tuned in. In addition, if they are the founder or CEO of a big name (multibillion-dollar valuation) company, they add a nice halo of credibility and savvy. Some large-cap companies may attract a thirty-year-old billionaire social media wunderkind. Small caps, private companies, and even tech start-ups might land a twenty-year-old globally renowned hacker or data analytics geek.

Onboarding

As a younger director joining an established board, as opposed to forming a new one, or as a member of the board adding this director, there are two primary areas of preparation that I recommend be addressed as part of the onboarding process: education and assimilation. There is also a third, less obvious one, which is attitude or perspective.

- **Education and information** The candidate will be well served by learning as much as possible about the company: its business, technology, customers, distribution channels, employees, facilities, culture, recent or current problems, opportunities, finances, competitors, company origin (if less than ten years or so old), vendors, banking/investment banking-legal-audit relationships, and the backgrounds of the board members and executives.

The board will likely have already done this homework on the candidate. I am a big fan of one-on-one (or max two-to-one) interviews between a candidate and all board members. It is unfortunate when a serious personality clash arises between a candidate and the one director that they did not meet. I feel that the days of everyone approving sight unseen a selection made by a small nominating committee or the CEO are long gone.

As part of the educational process, I always recommend that the final candidate (under NDA if necessary) review a selection of governance documentation. This can include previous board minutes, resolutions, current capitalization schedule, status of debt/debt holders, stock option plan and allocations (and any forms of synthetic equity or deferred compensation), and of course litigation.

When first joining a board I like to understand the board's assessment of primary risks, which are often found missing something material. If the freshman has not previously sat on a board then perhaps even some education or coaching on governance would be in order.

- **Assimilation** The assimilation of a new member should be made as smoothly as possible. The board is there to exercise its guidance and fiduciary responsibilities as a body, as well as individually. This is a continual process. Every ongoing board that is satisfactorily performing has a cadence, a rhythm, and a cultural process. Sometimes this cultural element is healthy and open, inviting productive discussions, and sometimes it is not.

There are a very limited number of circumstances when one new director can change this quickly — for example, if he or she represents a very large new investor. Under most other situations a new director is advised to first get in synch with the board's style. Unless a new director comes aboard with some mandated authority or control, the power to change a board's culture must be earned and awarded over time.

This assumes that the board's culture is a healthy one. Under some circumstances the addition of a new director can be used as a catalyst to begin the process of changing the culture. This is best done with a specific plan and under the guidance of the chairman or presiding director. In a board of directors, where every director has one vote, power and influence come primarily from respect and confidence, which are not gained quickly or easily. Smoothly entering the process facilitates your ability to build your credibility and fully understand the dynamics between the individual directors, and avoid stepping into deep *trouble*.

Diversity and Attitude

As we already discussed in the previous chapter, there are several facets to diversity; more than are commonly referenced. Most discussions revolve around a traditional three-dimensional view of diversity, namely race, gender, and age. In this case age almost always is referring to directors being too old, not too young. In today's ultra-competitive business climate, a time of *perfect knowledge* — where everyone knows just about everything that everyone else everywhere does, at just about the same time — the diversity issue should be about bridging the gap between the customers that provide your livelihood and the expertise and experience contained in the combined resources of the CEO, senior management team, and board of directors. More specifically, having on your board personnel resources that understand all aspects of your customers, your industry, and business in general. I suggest that this view of diversity also include a complementary set of professional skills, industry or domain expertise, demographic diversity, geographic representation — and yes, youth.

In each of these diversity categories, by definition, there exist corresponding attitudinal differences. This is no less true with an age difference. Those entering the digital age of advanced electronics and communications in their 50s will generally not view today's complex digital landscape the same as someone born in the 1990s. This is not good or bad, or better or worse, but just a fact.

This variation in viewpoints can either add immeasurable incremental material value to a board's oversight and strategic guidance, or it can entangle, confuse, strangle, and paralyze it. The key in my opinion is two-fold: each board member's ability to steadfastly focus on their fiduciary responsibility to the shareholders and the value of the enterprise, and their ability to collaboratively explore key issues, render informed decisions, and provide appropriate governance.

In Summary

The placement of a new director is always sensitive. If the new director is particularly young, this adds even more to the challenge for both the freshman director and the board. To the extent that each individual director, new and sitting, resolve to educate and inform themselves, and cooperate to meld their personalities and expertise, they will have the opportunity to deliver the highest level of governance and wisdom to their company.

Wanted: a thirty-year-old expert

I applaud companies whose boards are open and progressive enough to broaden their nominating criteria in this way. I believe that there are very good reasons to add youth to a board. I also believe that there are some critical categories of risk, opportunity, and diversity that may be best found in a younger person. It is also true that adding a thirty-something rock-star billionaire can accomplish all three, and add certain credibility to the company. However, look carefully at both the need, and available talent. Here are two contrasting examples, one real and the other fictitious:

• *Wal-Mart Stores Inc.: With 2016 revenues of over $480 billion it is a giant in the retail industry, it sells to billions of consumers of all ages, it has a high reliance on IT, it is highly affected by Internet/social media/mobility, it maintains large online databases of highly personal information, and it must embrace mobile applications. Can youth on the board ad value? Absolutely, and they have two young technology/Internet/social media executives on their board.*

• *Acme Power Co. (fictitious): A power industry player with $100 million in 2014 revenue, it sells large generators to utilities (and has under fifty customers), it has trailing-edge IT, it does have Internet-based applications, but no need for a social media presence, and has no online database or mobile technology. Why bother adding a young director?*

Chapter 11

Cybersecurity Responsibility

Over the last few years, cybersecurity risk has quickly risen to be the most dangerous, multi-dimensional risk faced by any organization. The cyber part of the term cybersecurity is fairly new, especially for companies, while the security part is an age-old problem for businesses. In terms of corporate governance, who has the ultimate fiduciary responsibility for this critical issue? The board, of course.

What is in This Chapter?

This chapter will briefly review the evolution of information technology security. It will give you a different perspective on the board's responsibilities, and highlight four of the most common board and management practices that are obsolete and need revision as boards address cyber security risks.

Most board discussions of cybersecurity focus on potential threats, protection and response scenarios, and questions the board should be asking. This is fine, but with the potential magnitude of this risk, proactive oversight really requires more.

There are four common governance and management practices that are long overdue for changes.

In 2011, as a director and the interim CEO of a cutting-edge cybersecurity software firm, I found it to be an eye-opening experience; even after over four decades in the information technology industry. I met high-level NSA and Pentagon officials, congressmen, senators, and top technology and security experts. I had run software companies before, but this was different. The urgency of the issues was frightening. The ongoing white hat (good guy) development of defensive cybersecurity software was losing ground to increasingly aggressive and well-backed black hat (bad guy) actors of all sorts. The chasm we are careening toward is global economic chaos. This situation requires an unparalleled concentrated, cooperative government-sponsored effort to advance state-of-the-art defensive capabilities, and the ubiquitous deployment of those solutions to stave off the disastrous potential economic and social consequences.

The Origin of IT

Definition: cy·ber ˈsībər/ *Adjective,* of, relating to, or characteristic of the culture of computers, information technology, and virtual reality. "the cyber age" Synonyms: electronic, digital, wired, virtual, web, Internet, Net, online.

The real key to understanding today's cyber challenges can be found in the definition of *cyber,* and actually relates to the words *wired, web, Net, online* and especially the *Internet* part.

In the 1960s, what we now call information technology (IT), the overall digital computer environment within a company, was referred to as 'data processing'. It then evolved into 'management information systems (MIS)', or just systems. In those early days everything was strictly 'offline'. Almost nothing was interconnected with digital communications links, and therefore, there was little risk of information being compromised electronically from external sources.

At that time, the bad guys had to physically gain access to the premises in order to steal anything; and that was a physical risk for a criminal. Today, most systems are connected to the Internet, which has brought about defining changes to information security. The Internet now delivers ubiquitous, widespread digital communications linkages between peoples, companies and governments; globally, in millionths of a second. A thief can now hack a U.S. company's digital information while sitting comfortably at an Internet café in Beijing.

This perspective is key for companies. This is not about legacy enterprise software. This is not about IT professionals focused on applications, databases, productivity, user priorities, or costs. This is not about automating operations to stay ahead of competition. A proprietary or custom solution is not even an option. No single company, especially an end-user enterprise, can afford, much less be successful, at developing the complex cutting-edge technology needed to defend against the global threats that exist today and will exponentially increase tomorrow.

If someone were to ask the CEO of Sony today, "Would you rather be investigated by the SEC for seriously having misstated your financial information for the last three years, or would you prefer to have your computer systems hacked?" What do you think he would answer?

In 1995, investment banking analyst J. Neil Weintraut first offered the phrase, 'The Internet changes everything!' At that time, who could foresee the full implications of that statement? Today even common citizens in undeveloped countries can detail many of those implications. Few who are in business, or watch television, or read a newspaper, can remain unaware of the reach or risk of Internet-borne threats. How can the existing bodies of corporate governance and organizational good practices catch up? Currently even best-in-class companies have not adequately demonstrated their acknowledgement of the magnitude of these technological issues in fundamental ways that relate to their corporate governance and management practices.

Four Obsolete Practices

To many observers, the lack of these simple changes can put the board's overall performance into question. A majority of American corporations continue to adhere to four legacy governance and management practices that are now decades out of date. Changing these dynamics would dramatically contribute to mitigating cybersecurity risk within a business.

1. The senior C-level technology officer should report directly to the CEO. Depending on the nature of a company this C-level position may be a Chief Information Officer - the CIO is focused on information technology, or a Chief Technology Officer – the CTO is usually responsible for the technology produced by the company or embedded in its products.

   There is an emergence of the Chief Security Officer or CSO. This normally represents a specialization in cybersecurity. This poisition rarely replaces a CTO or CIO, and often reports to one or the other.If they do not, the company is still viewing technology in general as a tool, not core to their survival, and they therefore only put cybersecurity on par with other risks, including misalignment of financial data.

   When C-level tech reports to the COO, it will be viewed as an operational tool; and if to the CFO, it will be viewed as a cost center and generator of data. If reporting to the president, it will be viewed on a slightly higher plane, but unless reporting is done directly to the CEO, it will not be allocated the respect and resources that will be required for the entity's survival, much less success.

Until the leader of the enterprise is directly educated and informed, and buys in, no real protective or business-driving adaptations of technology can be truly successful.

2. The potential consequences of cyber risk in terms of breadth, depth, and magnitude, demand a new standard of board committee oversight. Cybersecurity is a risk, of course. Therefore, with most corporate boards, oversight usually falls under the audit committee, which is typically chaired by a retired accounting firm audit partner or a retired CFO.

    Is cybersecurity really best assessed in a financial context only? In addition to financial risk, can this committee really understand the potential catastrophic impact on the brand, the customers, the employees, or the regulators? Does the committee have any members who possess digital credentials? It is time that risk and finance are separated and both receive the committee attention and expertise that they deserve.

3. The overriding importance of IT in business demands that boards recruit directors with appropriate qualifications. As with the audit committee, very few boards of non-technology companies contain members with IT expertise. Even sitting directors who are former high-level CEOs generally have not had direct hands-on experience managing the digital technology infrastructure that was the underpinning of their massive organizations.

    In today's board room, expertise from the political, educational, non-profit, financial, and C-suite sectors are well represented, yet there is little or no technology expertise—specifically broad, real-world technology experience.

4. The full board needs to directly hear from senior technology management as frequently as they do senior financial executives. I have observed that few boards get direct reports from the senior technology executive frequently enough. Many only get full technology reports once or twice a year.

    With the critical nature of cybersecurity, not to mention the impact of technology on operations and marketing, I believe that the board should get direct updates on a number of key issues relating to technology at every meeting. In addition, referencing the above point, when senior technical management reports through the CFO or COO, the nature of the information is generally diluted and filtered. This does a disservice to directors, who then have to ask more in-depth questions, since those executives generally will not have the needed technical grasp of the issues.

    What board does not see financial metrics and key performance indicators at every meeting? The digital engine at the heart of producing the products, generating the financial performance and information, and protecting the enterprise's hard assets and intellectual property deserves no less.

As with all risk, the responsibility for cybersecurity risk ultimately lays with the board. The ground rules have changed for risk in general and for cybersecurity specifically. Boards that pursue best governance practices should be aggressively moving toward the policies proposed above in order to fully understand the potential implications of today's risk landscape and to effectively guide management in appropriately mitigating their dangers.

In Summary

In general, until a company's governance and management infrastructure has adapted to, and integrated today's technology challenges, the boards are not fulfilling their fiduciary duties. Times have changed and threats to all aspects of company security – physical, digital, cyber, intellectual property, confidential records, employee/customer/vendor information, etc. – have dramatically increased and gotten more granular and more sophisticated. I believe that it takes an entirely new board mentality and approach to position today's companies to protect themselves.

Chapter 12

Non-Profit vs. For-Profit Boards - The Fundamental Difference.

Food for thought. What is the most fundamental difference between for-profit and non-profit boards of directors, which is never considered?

> **What is in This Chapter?**
>
> Some boards of non-profit organizations are exceptional. However, anyone who has altruistically given their time and served on one knows that the excellent ones are an exception. The majority of not-for-profit boards of directors are dysfunctional. This chapter explains the most fundamental reason why.

I attended a conference at a prestigious governance institute within the business school at a major University. One of the panels was on the differences between boards of non-profit and for-profit organizations. During the presentation a discussion ensued about what was the proper term a 'non-profit'. Do you call it a *501(c)(3)*, a non-profit, a not-for-profit, a community service organization, or a charitable organization?

The panel and audience tossed around a variety of terms. One participant noted that she had been on some boards of companies that should have been for-profit, but were in fact non-profit, e.g.

not profitable. Perhaps not-for-profit (NFP) would be better? Which term do you like? Regardless, since profitability is not the best differentiator between the two organizational categories, what is? More importantly, what is the most fundamental difference between the two that affects their respective governance? Why are there so many different governance models among NFPs? What difference between the two is the root cause of so much management and board issues among NFPs? Why is it almost always left un-addressed in the establishment and governance of these organizations that are such a vital part of our communities?

Ownership

In any company, public or private, you can name every single person or entity that owns shares (or units, percentages) in the enterprise - there legally must be a list. In any NFP, try to name one single owner. Or ask two people who *owns* the entity. If the ownership of a firm is the beneficiary of the fiduciary responsibilities of the board of directors that oversees the organization and, as commonly accepted, the board reports to the owners, then to whom does the board of a NFP actually report to?

You could argue that a government-related NFP, like a school district, is 'owned' by the citizens in that district. You could argue that an NFP such as United Way or Red Cross, or American Heart Association is 'owned' by everyone in the community. Or, you could argue that no one person or group 'owns' any of these.

In Summary

With any intended for-profit company, regardless of whether it is public or private, there is an actual list of the owners (or who owns shares). This list may have one name or 100,000, but there is a specific list. Therefore, it's clear in a public or private company exactly who the shareholders are, and therefore to whom the board owes its fiduciary responsibilities. However, with a 501 (c)(3), rarely are directors elected by anyone other than the board itself (although sometimes).

Frequently new board nominees are presented by other directors, or even the Managing or Executive Director/President/CEO. This has resulted in a certain lack of uniformity in NFP governance. Which has in turn led to an overwhelming number of dysfunctional NFP board situations, particularly in the case of younger or smaller organizations.

If a board that has the responsibility to oversee an organization, does not know who it reports to, and to whom it owes its fiduciary responsibility, how can it really determine, on an organizational and operational level, how a decision effects its stakeholders?

There are of course ways of clarifying this through bylaws, policies, communications, licensing requirements and more, however the issue needs to be identified and rectified in order to enable these valuable community service organizations to do the best job possible in delivering their benefits to the causes and people that need them.

Chapter 13

The Chairman: Who's in Charge Around Here?

Simply put, this is where the 'buck' stops for a board to achieve its fullest potential.

> **What is in This Chapter?**
>
> The chairman of the board has a real job. Here we will take a look at the most important duties of the chairman vs the CEO. It also outlines the variations of the role.

The chairperson of a corporate fiduciary board of directors generally leads the board meetings. Many see this person simply as the ceremonial head of the board. But besides presiding over Robert's Rules of Order, what is the chairman or chairwoman's real responsibility?

Well, stated irrevocably, they should be the senior arbitrar of fiduciary responsibility and behavior — in other words, the chair is where the 'board' buck stops.

Recently I was asked, "What makes a good chairman of the board?" The best answer is not a checklist of qualities or tasks, but rather an *outcome*. My response is that a good chairperson is a director who leads their board to continually be the best that it can be in executing its fiduciary duties to the shareholders, and in questioning and guiding management in the best interests of building enterprise value.

This goes beyond managing the meeting through the agenda items to also include taking proactive actions to add missing expertise to the board, removing any directors who are no longer adding substantial value to the board, and always presiding over all meetings in a manner that insures and protects an open, respectful, and thoughtful discussion of all matters before the board. A great chair must continue to maintain the respect, trust and confidence of the other directors, the management and the shareholders/owners.

While the chairperson presides over the company's board of directors' meetings and other activities, he or she will usually not have any executive responsibilities unless of course they are both the chairperson and CEO. Over the last few years, due to public encouragement, it has become best practice to separate these roles.

The CEO is, of course, a company's top decision-maker, and all other executives answer to him or her. The chairperson of a company is the head of its board of directors, with no executive reports. Any authority the chairperson possesses is strictly that which is stipulated by the company bylaws or bestowed by the board itself. The balance of power between the CEO and the chairperson is best viewed as supportive, yet also a check and balance system to insure that the strategy, operations and culture of the firm are consistently in the best interests of all the shareholders.

The basic varieties of chairs

There are several basic varieties of chairs:

- The *chairman or chairwoman who is not an employee.* The most traditional situation is a chair who has no executive functions. They may be an independent director or a former employee.

- The *chairperson who is also CEO*. This chair/CEO simply fills both roles simultaneously. They have the full responsibility and authority of both positions.
- The *executive chairperson*, who is an employee but is not CEO. This position is generally a full-time job, and they may have the chairmanship duties as well as some high-level or even other management responsibilities, but specifically not the CEO role.
- The *presiding or lead director*, who acts as the alternate or independent leader of the board if the CEO is also the official chair. When there is a chairman/CEO, best practices call for an independent board director to serve as a shadow or alternate or backup chair, primarily taking the board lead in situations where the CEO might have potential conflict of interest issues.

A matter of 'fit'

The job of all board members is to learn all about the business, the way it makes money, its risks, its people, its culture and values, and its customers, and to use their collective judgment and experience to oversee company matters on behalf of the shareholders. It is important to note that simply being qualified to sit on a particular company board does not make an individual suitable. In addition to matching their skills and experience, a good chair will also insure that their personality and interpersonal approach are a good fit with the company and board cultures. A good chair can take the lead when needed, step into the background when necessary, and always keep the fiduciary obligations and constructive goals of the company in sight. As once stated by Jack Krol, former chairman and CEO of DuPont Co., "You want someone who has the conviction of their opinions, but is collaborative with other directors."

One of the things that you eventually realize if you are on a well-chaired board is that all the opinions around the table are not the same, i.e., in agreement. As a result, not all board votes are, nor do they need to be, unanimous. The most important goal should be that all reasonable relevant aspects of the issue have been appropriately surfaced and explored. Has the board thoughtfully and respectfully probed all the details and drawn out the broadest range of alternatives, solutions, and possible actions that would most benefit the organization? Based on my experience, my highest praise goes to chairpersons who possess the courage to embrace the tough, even unpopular, decisions and actions, in the interest of the enterprise.

A chairman's fate at the hands of a founder

A few years ago a friend of mine declined a board seat I offered him. He had just retired as the CFO of a $30 billion public company. He had reported to the founder-chairman-CEO. My friend told me that his boss had decided to split the chairman/CEO roles in an effort to respond to investor pressure, and he named my friend as chairman of the board while he retained the CEO title.

Some years passed and eventually the founder stepped down and replaced himself as CEO. When he relinquished the CEO title, he re-assumed the chairmanship title.

Upon reading about this in the business press, I sent my friend an email asking him if this meant that he might not have to work as hard, and perhaps he would now be able to consider sitting on another board. I got a chuckle when I received a quick response: "Sorry, Dennis. He assumed the chairmanship from me, and he has now elected me as vice chairman . . . but I'm still doing all the work."

In Summary

In conclusion, in my view no matter how exceptional, qualified and diverse a board may be, without the leadership of a strong, skilled and well grounded chairperson it risks not achieving its fullest potential at best, and severe dysfunction at worst.

Chapter 14

Director Qualities – the Most Needed, yet Least Named Qualities for a Great Board Member

There are some qualities for great directors that are seldom specified. This is a personal top-five list of the most needed — yet least identified — qualities for an outstanding board director.

What is in This Chapter?

There are many different qualifications that boards look for when filling out their director's matrix. Some have to do with demographics, gender, and extend to include management skills, job specialties and industry/domain expertise. This chapter will explore five of the most important characteristics that are rarely found on the matrix.

It is the norm for boards to compile a matrix of the key mix of skills and qualifications needed in directors to best guide the company going forward. A matrix highlights those attributes that are already represented by current directors and those that are desirable in prospective board candidates. Typically, the named categories include job skills such as CEO or financial expertise, and specific industry domain experience. These will often be overlaid with some additional unique skills and diversity goals. Sometimes a matrix will even contain broad character traits such as 'cultural compatibility' or 'leadership.' However, there are a number of traits that can be critical to a board's success but are not often listed in any matrix.

A Simple yet Effective Tool

Whether it is formally written, which is advisable, or just a verbal discussion, a matrix of desirable board director skills, experience, and other qualifications is a simple yet effective tool in identifying which boxes you already have checked and which are best targeted in a new director.

I have participated in several board symposiums, which have all arrived at the same conclusion — that many a company's greatest failures can be traced to a dysfunctional board. These discussions have also consistently come to the conclusion that a frequent cause of board dysfunction is personality conflicts between directors. Today's complex fast moving global business environment requires a high-performance board in order to maximize the success of any enterprise. Yet in spite of the direct link between performance and the personal communications styles and personality traits of board members, I have never seen any of these personal attributes specifically identified in a qualifications matrix.

Having had the privilege of sitting on many corporate boards over the last four-plus decades, I have observed and learned from over 250 fellow directors. Along the way I have developed my own top five list of the most important qualifications for an outstanding board director. A board can function well in executing its fiduciary responsibilities even if it is missing some specific skills or experience; however, it can be completely disrupted at a key point by just one rogue director having one heavy-handed character trait, especially if no one else on the board possesses the personality or authority to rein him or her in.

Examples might be:

- Someone who talks too much, repeating what was already stated numerous times (hijacks or filibusters the discussion), or
- One who daydreams or falls asleep (disrespectful and not adding value), or
- Is overly argumentative (polarizes members and fosters dissension).

Unless another member, preferably the chairman or presiding/lead independent director, has a personality that can appropriately counter it, that one negative director can potentially sidetrack a critical discussion, negatively impacting the business.

My top-five most desirable character traits. Come up with your own, and formally or informally add it into your board's evaluation and nominating processes.

Courage: The Only No. 1

There may be many opinions on ranking the importance of various character traits that could contribute to a board's performance and ability to work together to provide a truer execution of its fiduciary duties. Weighting might even vary depending on the composition of any given board and the current circumstances of the firm. However, I have two important observations: only negative situations expose the nitty gritty soul of a board, and in those instances no characteristic for any director will prove more vital than *courage*. All others pale in comparison to the courage of a single director who is willing to voice the unstated truth of a situation, the unpopular alternative, the feared conclusion, or the out-of-the-box creative idea that could right the ship. Others may sense that action is necessary, but typically most will not muster the selfless moral strength to risk ridicule, or even rejection, to boldly articulate the unpopular deed.

Leadership and courage are not always present together, although they can be. Does the CEO have to be terminated? Does a business unit have to be closed? Does the company need to accept or reject a financing or acquisition offer? Should the firm publicly admit or not admit to some grievous mistake or regulatory infraction? Every seasoned director can recall similar confrontations. Was there at least one board member who possessed the courage to step out on the limb and articulate the necessary truths? If so, did it likely avert even worse consequences?

Candor: For Frictionless Dialog

My second choice is less obvious, and is multifaceted. In many informal chats with board members from other companies, someone always decries to some degree their board's politics. I attribute the politics to a lack of candor on the part of one or more directors. Without the presence of candor, board members often resort to deception and behind-the-scenes maneuvers to accomplish their objectives.

Malicious or not, manipulative behavior — not clearly stating one's position and reasoning, or a lack of transparency among board colleagues — will at best waste precious time, energy and money. At worst it can paralyze rational, effective decision-making and precipitate a catastrophe. This is not about teamwork (that comes a little later), but rather each individual's ability to be forthright in the best and highest interest of the enterprise.

Humor: The Most Underrated

I will reluctantly admit that in retrospect I regret that I have not always lived up to my own standards in courage or candor, particularly in my youth. Humor, on the other hand, has always been a personal strength. It can be a highly underrated technique in a traditionally stodgy corporate boardroom full of self-important, know-it-all business chieftains (present company excluded, of course).

I have prevailed in board debates far more times with humor than I have with logic. The beauty of humor is that only one person need be able to highlight the irony or silliness of the situation, or diffuse conflict with a well-placed and relevant joke or analogy. Everyone else simply need only appreciate it and participate. The discussion can then proceed again with significantly less tension and resistance, thereby dialing up everybody's willingness to listen to one another. Humor tends to draw the group closer together for common purpose.

Inquisitiveness: Uncovering the Detail

For many years one of my top reasons for joining a board has been the quality of the other directors. Personally, I like to meet them in advance if possible. I have always sought the opportunity to hone my governance skills and judgment by watching and learning from others. I have one board colleague of fourteen years who served on the boards of General Motors, Raytheon, Hewlett-Packard, Hughes Electronics, Harvard and others. While I am proud that he has learned one thing from me — how not to always wear a suit and tie to board meetings — I have learned many priceless lessons from him.

My favorite is *inquisitiveness*. We have all likely learned to beware of the director who enthusiastically expounds on every topic, even if it has already been well covered by others. However, my colleague has taught me how valuable it is to listen to a question asked by the board member who rarely speaks. He will often start with the phrase, "May I ask a dumb question?" What typically follows is anything but, rather, it is a precisely articulated inquiry that pierces to the heart of the issue, and often opens up a whole new vista for discussion. A well-placed, well-phrased inquiry can sometimes work as effectively as humor to break a downward spiral in a debate. It is questions like those, from colleagues like him that can propel a board to great moments.

Collaborative: There Is No 'I' in board

A high performance board is a team sport. At any given moment even one 'showboat' member can derail an otherwise productive dialog. Among any group of accomplished business leaders there can sometimes be a tendency for anyone to feel compelled to take charge. The inclination to collaborate may not be their first response. The best directors are those who can subdue their own egos, and who have nothing to prove; those who can blend their talents with their fellow board members' for the good of their enterprise.

In Summary

This list of traits is not comprehensive. One might also consider logic, decisiveness, intelligence, judgment, integrity, discernment, vision, creativity, and more. I encourage all board nominating and governance committees, for both public and private company boards, to consider the value of articulating some of these in your requirements document and screening for them when you interview for new candidates.

Chapter 15

Compensation Models and Metrics: It's about More Than Money

What would it take to recruit a board member who has recently termed off of the boards of four Fortune 100 companies – probably making about $1,000,000/year in combined total compensation? Oh, and your company is early-stage, in bleeding edge tech R&D, has virtually no revenue, continuing losses, and pays no cash fees.

What about recruiting someone who currently sits on the boards of three Fortune 100 companies, one as presiding director, and your firm has under $4MM in annual revenue, and also pays no fees?

How could you ever convince the retired original founder, and former chairman and CEO (with a very high net worth) of a hot public $40 billion market cap tech company with $6B in revenue, to join the board of your private company – regardless of revenue – when you are only paying a modest cash fee and no equity?

Could you convince the CEO of one of the country's leading information technology research and advisory companies to join your board rather than that of 3M Corporation?

There are many circumstances where highly qualified, experienced, accomplished individuals chose to join a for profit private company fiduciary board of directors, for very little or even no cash compensation.

If and when a qualified and suitable individual agrees to join your fiduciary board of directors (or advisory board for that matter), it is not – and nor should it be – about the money. Compensation should certainly be fair in regard to the amount of time and liability involved, and in regard to what the firm can reasonably afford, however, that is rarely the key to why a world-class, highly experienced, and successful individual would agree to devote their time and priceless experience to helping you make your company more successful. There has to be something more.

What might that be for your company? What is the secret sauce?

What is in This Chapter?

Compensation is frequently a thorny issue for those considering forming a board. This chapter shows there are considerations beyond money. We review compensation models – the basics, as well as a discussion of the criteria for those evaluating joining a board. We review a number of models, and get detailed specifics and opinions from ten different seasoned board directors.

Compensation Model

Most of what I have read on board compensation, public or private, includes annual surveys, quantitative statistics and comparisons of comp levels across industries, geographies, and company revenue ranges. These are usual groupings. This may be useful on an annual basis for a frame of reference and comparison purposes, however, beyond the stats it does not offer much insight into building a compensation model, or the various creative styles and balances that are available to be tailored to specific circumstances. In this chapter, I felt it would be more worthwhile to focus on some insights into the strategies, approaches, and considerations of board compensation, rather than just numbers.

Board Acceptance Criteria

In my experience, having personally nominated and on-boarded hundreds of directors, and interviewed many more, I have found there to be eight basic reasons why someone will accept an offer to join a board. The priority of these is very subjective and varies from person-to-person.

1. **Who** - *Who else is on the board? Would a candidate like to serve with them?*
2. **Opportunity/Risk** – *Is the company successful, profitable, growing, or a little troubled; or is it a turnaround? Is it properly capitalized? What is the overall risk? Is D&O coverage adequate? Would one learn or experience something new and interesting, even exciting?*
3. **Business** – *What Business or industry is the company in? Is it interesting? Can one learn something new from it?*
4. **Workload** – *How much time and effort will be involved? How many meetings? How much preparation will be necessary prior to meetings?*
5. **Where** – *Where is the company located? Where will the meetings be? Would any required travel be interesting? How much travel will be required?*
6. **First timer** – *Is this the first real board invitation? Can it be used as a steppingstone?*
7. **Secret desire** – *Is there something about this board or this company situation that fulfills some deeper emotional or intellectual desire? Is there some prestige, or chance to make a meaningful difference in the industry or world?*
8. **Compensation** – *Is the compensation offered acceptable, relative to all the other above factors?*

I have found that compensation has consistently been the least important factor in getting the director you want, and just as subjective as any of the others.

Good Enough for the Best

Even the most experienced authorities on board compensation will disagree on one point or another about recruiting board members – there is no single answer or approach. When I first published Chapter 3 of this book, *Finding directors*, as an article in Directors & Boards Magazine (*Finding directors for the smaller and early-stage company*, Q2 2012) I was surprised at how few calls I received from companies searching for directors. I was equally surprised at the large number of calls I received from individuals all over the world who were interested in being connected to board director opportunities. There is no shortage of talent. The trick is in getting the very best board members your company can possibly attract.

Compensation Basics

One point that almost everyone agrees on is consistency. The base compensation structure and fees for a board should be the same for all directors qualifying for compensation, based on their relative responsibilities and liabilities. The term *qualifying* refers to whether the company bylaws and board policy grant or deny fees to management directors, or directors who are or represent large shareholders, whether they are directors due to courtesy, or based on preferential stock ownership terms.

Within this 'policy' of consistency, the fee model that I have found works the best is to set the base fee at a level that is acceptable to the *most valuable* director you have or hope to attract – regardless if it is a base cash fee, cash incentive, equity, or some combination of all. If the combination works for your most desirable director, then it should be sufficient to attract and keep others.

We will discuss specific payment formats and amounts below, but beyond that there is one more variable. Although it is not required, most often additional compensation is provided for a variety of board responsibilities including chairman, lead or presiding director (the preferred title for independent directors when the chairman is a sitting executive of the firm or retired but still paid a full-time salary), selected committee membership and committee chairpersons.

Within the above parameters, compensation is usually split between a fixed, or base fee, and additional compensation for additional risk/responsibilities. The base fees cover the individual's normal board service. Then there may be 'add-ons' for additional responsibilities, risks or time. These can all be paid in the form of any combination of cash (current or deferred), ownership shares (restricted or not), stock options (generally non-qualified), phantom or synthetic options, economic units, and more, including perks like travel, automobiles, and more.

Note: Some or all of the cash can be deferred, and the stock options are typically 'deferred' through a scheduled vesting over time.

In addition, there can also be additional incentives for the directors. Although these can be individually based, they are usually based on the overall success of the enterprise. These elements can include all the same instruments as above. Often they are linked to metrics considered important by the company's owners – for example net profit, return on capital, market share, strategic initiatives, and more.

Compensation Policies

Depending on the variety of boards and ownership scenarios one has had experience with, they may be aware of this information, however, it never hurts to review a few more basics.

Compensation will vary depending on the following:

a. Is a director independent or are they a founder/company executive, a venture capital or private equity investor? Unless they are unaffiliated with the company, independent, you may or may not pay them fees.

b. Does the company have plans for a liquidity event at some point? If so, how would the firm like to balance its board fees between cash and equity?

c. How experienced are your independent directors? Freshman directors may be less concerned about fees; however, I still recommend parity among all directors, as discussed above.

Typically, compensation would only be paid to directors who were independent (non-employee). It is not typical to pay any fees, beyond expenses, to directors who are on the management team, to large investors or representatives of large investors (unless under special arrangements), or who are on the board representing an ownership class that has a board seat as part of their preferred shareholder class rights.

Large investors would be optional. Paying fees to these types of investors is often seen as excessive since they are there representing specific interests or are already likely being paid directly by their sponsors. However, this is completely up to the board and shareholders, and can be changed at any time with an appropriate vote. One additional note, in my book it is considered improper for directors representing large shareholders to receive special payments other than their normal salary, for sitting on a board. This is usually an issue only associated with private equity firms.

Stake in the ground

Just to establish a reasonable starting point let's talk some numbers. Keep in mind that board fees generally trend up over time – along with most everything else. However, that is not a rule. Fees also tend to vary by geography, industry, and private companies vs. publicly traded ones, as was noted earlier.

Let's establish a reasonable general set of conditions that might represent base fees for an independent director of a private company in an industry that is not at the extremes of evolutionary or revolutionary change, is not early-stage, is modestly profitable, and is located in reasonably well-developed business geography. A mid-range fee, with these conditions, may range from no cash/all equity to all equity/no cash, or any combination.

In this generalized scenario, compensation might reasonably fall in the range of $24,000 - $36,000 in cash fees per year for profitable firms with $25MM or less in annual revenue. This can ramp up to $75,000 for firms up to $100MM in annual revenue, and up to $150,000 for firms at $1B or above in revenue. Keep in mind that this is intended for non-public companies, especially where the risks are minimized by their private ownership.

These fees might be paid in a variety of formats including an annual retainer, or per-meeting. In addition to any base cash fee, there might be a slight premium paid to an independent chairman or lead director, as well as the chairperson of the audit or other time-consuming committee responsibilities.

In companies that foresee a potential eventual liquidity event of some type (IPO or sale) there may also be restricted stock or stock options generally equal to between a quarter to half percent of the outstanding shares of the company, for companies in the smaller range. However, it can often be even more. I have seen up to five percent. The equity percentage goes down as the company size increases. If the ownership of the firm does not want to grant equity, an incentive component can be structured as profit sharing, synthetic equity (value tracking formula), 401(k), or other performance related instruments.

It should be noted that there are multiple ways of calculating the outstanding shares of any corporation. The variations include counting or not certain categories of non-vested or non-exercised granted stock options, or restricted stock.

Equity awards would trend down in a more mature or larger company closer to liquidity, or one having a higher perceived fair market value. It will generally trend up in the case of an earlier-stage firm, a smaller size or lower valuation, or one perceived as riskier.

I believe that any less than the above examples may run the risk of being under market, and anything more may be considered to be approaching overly generous – although, for the right individuals, their on-going contributions could well be worth it.

Ultimately it depends on what the desired directors are willing to accept, and what the board, in exercising its fiduciary responsibilities on behalf of all shareholders deems appropriate. I will caution the reader that this methodology, and these representative numbers, may be some of the most controversial information contained in this book. No subject will elicit a wider range of strong opinions. I believe that any opinion from someone who has served on at least two for-profit boards is valid. This is one of the most subjective topics in the area of corporate governance. Ultimately it is about whatever compensation scheme succeeds in attracting and retaining the best possible directors to advise, support and oversee your company, and work with management to build enterprise value.

Thoughts Directly from the Boardroom

One of the most valuable contributions that boards can make to any enterprise is perspective – surfacing all the relevant alternatives or approaches for any decision that might face management. I find this review of informed decisions to be important in many other situations as well.

My own board experience spans almost five decades, and approaching sixty for profit boards, including several public ones, in several industries, although mostly technology. In order to present my readers with the most expanded representation of viewpoints, I have reached out to a number of very seasoned board governance colleagues. All have deep experience in an exceptional range of corporate settings. Few have sat on less than three corporate boards, and some have been on dozens. Some are noted academic experts. Several have spoken widely on the topic of governance and boards. Collectively they have sat on dozens of different Fortune 100 boards, small-caps, mid-caps, large-caps, both public and private, large multi-generational family businesses, private equity owned, large multi-national companies, and a multitude of early-stage and start-ups including numerous financed by major east and west coast venture capital firms. Some of my colleagues have long illustrious careers individually providing services on dozens of boards – including some of the most well-known and respected companies in the world.

I asked each one to answer this question.

"Would you be willing to pen your thoughts on board director compensation? Would you write between 100 and 500 words on your personal thoughts? Virtually anything you wish.

You may talk about how to motivate directors, what currency to use: base fees, incentive fees, committee fees, cash, stock, deferred comp, synthetic/phantom equity, etc. You may give any opinions you like and feel would help someone trying to form the best board they can in the true spirit of corporate governance and fiduciary responsibilities. You may talk about the compensation differences between fiduciary boards and advisory boards, you may discuss segmenting compensation by committee participation or meeting attendance, and you may, of course, talk about actual dollar amounts if you wish. What is your philosophy about board compensation?

Simply remember that the focus of the book is boards for private for-profit companies of any size, not public ones and not non-profits. Please let your vast experience and opinions shine through."

With nothing more to go on, each person below shares here their unique perspective on what is personally important to them about board compensation - how they view it, how they approach it, what they feel works, and more. In some cases, their comments include both public company and non-profit boards as well.

Note: For the most part, their comments are unedited. I used a very light editing touch - just enough to provide continuity and readability. I have also included is a very brief biography of each.

Candid Insights

Tom Everhart

First, thanks for asking. However, I probably can be of little help, since I have never helped set board compensation, nor used it as a determination of whether or not I was willing to serve.

Like most directors, if I think the enterprise is worthwhile, the people are honorable, and the results will benefit society, I am likely to accept an invitation to serve on a board if I have time available. So here are a few words to hopefully help you out.

Dr. Thomas E. Everhart
California Institute of Technology,
President Emeritus
Boards of:
- General Motors
- Hewlett-Packard
- Agilent Technologies
- Hughes Electronics
- Raytheon
- California Institute of Technology Board of Trustees
- Secretary of Energy Advisory Board - Chairman
- Harvard Board of Overseers
- KCET, the Los Angeles public television station

Private companies generally don't have money to compensate directors, unless they become large, like Koch Industries. I have no input for large companies such as these. For smaller companies, fighting for their fiscal lives, stock options seem to be the usual method of compensation, and this makes sense to me. Some smaller companies pay travel expenses. I personally have found that other members of the board are interested in equitable compensation using stock options, and try to be fair to all members of the board using this method of (potential) compensation.

On large public boards, there seem to be various methods of compensation (as can be seen by reading annual reports). These include cash retainer, cash meeting fees, stock retainer, options to purchase stock at some future time, or some combination of these. The values of this compensation must be meaningful to get good people to serve, but should not be so large that it is their primary source of income. In my experience, people serve on boards for a variety of reasons, and financial compensation probably ranks rather far down on the list of factors that motivate their service.

Bill Gross

I don't have a lot of value to add around compensation, as most of the boards I serve on are private and most of our positions are uncompensated. Most of the directors are investors and their upside is from their stock holding. In "some" cases a board member may get about 0.5% to 1%, vesting over four years. But typically they don't get cash or equity board compensation.

Bill Gross
Founded Idealab, Chairman of the Board and Chief Executive Officer, Founder of a number of other companies including Solar Devices, GNP Loudspeakers Inc., GNP Development (acquired by Lotus Development Corporation), Knowledge Adventure (acquired by Havas Vivendi),
Boards of approximately 20 of idealab!'s public and private companies, including:
- GoTo.com
- NetZero

- Ticketmaster Online-CitySearch
- Overture
- Cooking.com
- WeddingChannel
- eToys
- .tv
- Pet.net
- Shopping.com
- Tickets.com
- Commission Junction
- Answers.com
- Newbury Networks
- California Institute of Technology and Art Center College of Design Trustees

Ray Hemmig

The best directors I have worked with, all have wanted some form of compensation for their time and their efforts. And I can easily say that most of the time, the value of their advice and their service was well in excess of the amount compensated.

Board members usually spend considerable time working not only at meetings or prepping for them. The statistics say that board members spend between 200 and 400 hours a year in their board roles. Many say that these numbers are low. I have observed that the good outside directors also spend

Raymond C. Hemmig
Founder, Chairman of the Board and Chief Executive Officer, General Partner and Chairman of Retail and Restaurant Growth Capital, L.P.

- Buffet Partners, Chief Operating Officer; Executive Vice President; Chief Executive Officer; and Lead Director, Executive and Non-Executive Chairman of the Board

Boards of:

- Elizabeth Arden Holdings
- Furr's Restaurant Group, Inc. - Chairman
- Restoration Hardware Inc.
- ACE Cash Express Inc. - Chairman
- QualServ Corporation

some of their intellectual thought
time thinking about company
issues, and trying to help the
enterprise that they are serving.

- On The Border Cafes, Inc.
- Full House Resorts Inc.
- NASC Enterprises

If an owner of a private company wants to add appropriate talent to the entity's board of directors he has to consider many things. In addition to choosing the skill set, advice perspective, and experience basis, the owner needs to try to align the incentive interests of that outside board member with the same interest of the owners of the enterprise – grow the company and shareholder value.

The best way to do that is to consider a form of director compensation for that outside person in either cash or equity, and more usually both.

Size Matters, for a private company that is. Larger (>$500MM) private companies usually utilize compensation consultants and their research typically states that the private board compensation is parallel to similarly sized public companies. Board comp can top $500K per year in larger public, and some large private entities. Whether the fees are really worth the advice and service is not a topic of this section. However, the comp range on smaller sized private companies in my experience is much more varied and creative.

I have seen that board members in small to mid-size private companies receive an average cash comp of $20-$75K per year. Paid either in an annual retainer (usually quarterly) or in a combination of retainer and per meeting fees. Those usually total to about the same average cash comp. Some even pay additional fees for specific committees.

The comp experts say that the best percentage of cash and equity compensation split is ~50/50%. Private companies (< $250MM in revenue) generally pay at the higher end of the cash scale and also provide a form of longer-term equity compensation as well. Most equity packages for directors vest over three to five years, and therefore help the *owner align the interests of the board with the owners of the business. Smaller companies (<$50MM) may find themselves with tighter SG&A or cash issues; therefore, they try to make up the average cash comp ($25-$50K) solely with a form of equity instead. While the amount of the equity compensation (shares/units/etc.) will vary, the best rule of thumb I have found is to create a value proposition for the outside director, based on a multiple of 3-5X their annual cash comp, using Black/Scholes or some other form of projectable equity value analytics.*

What you want is when a member's board service is completed; they can look at a value creation that is equivalent to their time and efforts. In private board compensation, you usually get what you pay for. If that is not priced at market or relevant to the particular outside director - remember the old adage, 'free advice is worth the price.'

Bob Kueppers

There is an inverse relationship among several relevant factors on the issue of private director compensation: the size of the company, the contribution of directors in terms of their involvement with the business and director compensation.

The following seems to be true based on the data:

- *The larger the company, the higher the overall director compensation.*
- *Director involvement with the business (beyond the*

Robert J. Kueppers
Former Senior Partner, Deloitte LLP Global Regulatory and Corporate Governance, member firm of Deloitte Touche Tohmatsu Limited

- Led the Deloitte Center for Corporate Governance
- Former Deputy CEO, Managing Partner of Deloitte's Center for Corporate Governance, U.S.
- Leader of Regulatory & Public Policy, Deloitte's Chief Risk Officer, Senior Technical Partner, leader of SEC Services & Independence group.
- Recognized by the National Association of Corporate Directors (NACD) Directorship

minimal typical directors' governance role) tends to be greater for smaller, less developed companies.

magazine as one of the top 100 influential professionals in corporate governance and in the boardroom - 2009, 2012, 2013, and 2014.

Boards of:

- United Way of New York City - Chairman
- SEC Historical Society - Founding Trustee, past President, and Chairman
- Committee for Economic Development - Trustee and Executive Committee member

This suggests that the value brought by a slate of involved directors to private companies results in compensation that is not commensurate with the value provided. Alternatively, it could lead to the conclusion that large public companies are 'overpaid' relative to the value they provide.

I do not think it is necessary to determine which conclusion is the right one. Rather, it is worthwhile to consider how to appropriately compensate directors to attract and retain the right directors to private companies.

My suggestion as a viable model for private company directors is as follows:

- *For Advisory Board members, compensation should be cash commensurate with the commitment of time of the members*
- *For a fiduciary board, I think the best model is a combination of cash and equity in whatever form makes sense for the situation. I continue to believe that a combination comp package serves the dual purpose of allowing the board members to share in success through the equity and cash shows that you want them on the board.*

I recommend this with full recognition that many private companies have structures and families or founders that make the equity piece difficult. But this is all about making the leap to a valued structure for a private firm. I am fine with extra comp for an independent chair and certain committee chairs. I think that should be in cash.

- *Generally, I am not in favor of "per meeting" fees. If there is a crisis, the commitment of board members on the front end anticipates that certain circumstances could arise. I am not in favor of separately compensating directors to help according to a pre-determined schedule. I would rather deal with that after resolution if warranted.*

Gerry Czarnecki

Obviously, the appropriate level of the compensation will be influenced by factors such as business size, complexity, type of board (fiduciary vs. advisory), director experience, and the state of the business (stable vs. troubled). That said, my experience with private companies as a board member and as a consultant really has always been that the board compensation has been generally structured in a way to parallel the compensation of directors in similarly sized public companies. That is where the data is, as most information on private companies, is just that, private. Hence, the only metric that is generally available is that which is compiled by organizations like compensation consultants to public companies.

Gerald M. Czarnecki
Senior Managing Director & Executive Producer, Ventureland Productions, LLC
Chairman & CEO of The Deltennium Group,
Former Chairman and Founder of Snowden Hill, and Chairman, President & CEO of Honfed Bank
Boards of:
- State Farm Insurance
- State Farm Bank
- State Farm Fire & Casualty
- Jack Cooper Holdings
- MAM Software Group, Inc., - Chairman
- Aftersoft, Inc. – Chairman

Tony LeVecchio

I've always felt that private company board compensation first must be tailored to what the company can afford both in stock and in cash. For some private companies in the early stage, the majority of the board compensation must be in equity. They can't afford to risk their cash when they are at a critical time in the company's development, even though they need sage advice

> **Anthony J. LeVecchio**
> President and Principal of The James Group, Inc.
> Former Senior Vice President and Chief Financial Officer of VHA Southwest Inc.
> Boards of:
> - Legacy Texas Financial Group, Inc. LTXB - Chairman
> - Ascendant Solutions
> - UniPixel – Co-chairman
> - DG Fast Channel
> - Microtune, Inc.

and guidance both in strategy, risk, and corporate governance.

A more established private company would still have the same requirements as a young company but probably have more maturity, more consistent and predictable performance and would pay a higher percentage of board compensation in cash. This is especially the case when a private company is closely held and there is no plan for a liquidating or selling event. In this situation, while the equity may increase in value, lack of liquidity options require this larger private company to focus more on cash compensation.

I've never been a proponent for phantom (equity) or complicated calculations of equity with a cash conversion feature. To me, it just doesn't work and gets too confusing setting relative values that become very difficult and tricky.

Brian Bonner

Companies seeking to recruit high caliber board members should first focus on the type of people that are joining the board. Having one or two high-powered members makes recruiting strong candidates much easier since folks want

> **Brian Bonner**
> Former Vice President & Chief Information Officer, Texas Instruments Inc.
> Boards of:
> - Daseke Inc.
> - Copper Mobile, Inc.
> - Gemini Israel Funds

to know that there is a level of excellence already on the board. That is primary. Next, the topic of compensation needs to be addressed.

If the board is non-public, a portion of the compensation should be in cash. This shows that the company is willing to spend and invest in a board just as they would for excellent outside counsel. The company should also create the ability to share its success as well. This can be done by the issuance of stock options. A good target here is half to two percent of the outstanding share count.

Another approach is to offer the board member the opportunity to buy preferred stock (or synthetic/phantom stock). This would convert to common at an agreed to ratio at some trigger. This stock could also pay a dividend. This serves two purposes. It again links the board to the company's performance with the upside of the common stock. It helps the company raise needed cash and also showcases the quality of their pre-IPO investors.

Marc Hodak

The goals of compensation are the same in every company all the time: pay what you have to in order to get the talent you want; don't pay any more than you have to. All the rest

> **Marc Hodak**
> Founder of Hodak Value Advisors (HVA), a research and consulting firm advising senior executives and boards on finance and compensation issues.

is details. The details, of course, are important. Cash or equity? Guaranteed or contingent? Current or deferred? How you answer those items can affect the attractiveness and cost-effectiveness of your compensation program.

Money is inherently problematic when it comes to good directors. You can always draw people you don't want or need to be on your board with money. In fact, many people you don't want or need would join a for-profit board for free. The kind of

Professor of Corporate Governance at NYU's School for Professional and Continuing Studies Center for Finance, Law and Taxation
Visiting Lecturer at the University of St. Gallen in Switzerland.
Formerly led value-based management implementation projects for Stern Stewart & Co
Published numerous articles in various journals on corporate governance, value-based management, transfer pricing, and organizational design
Developed seminars at Wharton and MIT

talent you want may not need money. And if they are still focused on earning money, you may not be able to afford them. Fortunately, money is rarely the main draw for good, prospective board members. They want to help you or your idea succeed. They want to stay engaged in interesting or inspiring business problems. You should take advantage of these draws first. Money should be used just to 'top off the tank'.

Regardless of the financial situation of your independent directors, you should offer some cash award that at least compensates them for their time. If they are putting in thirty or forty hours a year for you, $30,000 or $40,000 in fees should be a good start. Bigger companies may need more time and, therefore, more fees. Even if they are willing to serve for less, you should still pay them the equivalent of a professional partner's wages in order to compensate them fairly for their service. This lets them know that you take their service seriously and that they should, in turn, take their service seriously. Volunteers or folks taking token payments can always rationalize not 'giving their all' to an endeavor.

One constraining factor is the fact that you need to pay all of your independent directors the same. I say that as someone who normally has no problem differentiating people according to their relative contributions with steep differences in pay. A well-run board is a team. If they belong on your team, you want them to work together to help you focus on your business. You don't want to get into the second business of trying to distinguish which of your directors is contributing relatively more or less. Whatever you might possibly gain from accurately distinguishing their relative contributions you will more than lose by the perception of unfairness. This is especially true if you have a diverse board in terms of age, gender, ethnicity, etc. If you have one person you need to have who was a former secretary of X, and who will simply not join for less than $150,000, then hire them as a consultant, not as a board member.

It was once fashionable to pay meeting or attendance fees. These are unnecessary and increasingly irrelevant. While it's always better to have meetings face-to-face, meetings via videoconference or meetings via phone are perfectly acceptable, and people can contribute when they are not physically there. If they repeatedly don't show up, get them off the board.

Fees in public companies are also often differentiated by committee type or committee role, e.g., chairperson. This practice is bleeding into private companies because of the mistaken belief that public company practices often represent 'best practices'. These differences began as a function of the different level of risk and scrutiny, as well as work, associated with these different board roles. None of these differences apply to a private company. If you are Chairwoman of the Audit Committee in a private company, you can worry about whether the numbers are right. If you are Chairman of the Compensation Committee, you can worry if the pay is right. The threshold for duty of care and loyalty in either of these instances is not that high if you have the right support for your decisions. But you don't have to worry about the SEC or proxy advisors or major institutional investors (who aren't otherwise on your board) second-guessing your judgments, and potentially dragging you through the press or the courts. Keep it simple. Unless you have a particularly large and complex firm, pay everyone the same.

If your strategy contemplates the sale of your company or some similar liquidity event, then you may be able to excite a valuable, potential board member with equity. In fact, there might be some people who are more interested in equity than cash. Since you're a private company, you don't want to mess with your capital structure with numerous or frequent grants. But if you can pull it off, equity is a perfectly acceptable substitution or, if necessary, supplement for their pay. This is one place where my 'don't discriminate' rule can be modified. If a one-time grant to a well-connected, former CEO in your industry is needed to get them on board, go ahead. Again, if they are asking for a lot of total compensation for their skills or connections, hire them as a consultant, not as a board member.

Jim Ethier

Our non-employee fiduciary directors (whether family or independent) receive a quarterly meeting fee. Should they be asked for additional service, the same daily fee is applicable. Additionally, these directors share in the company reward plan at the same level as the CEO and the Chairman

The company reward plan covers all employees and is based on ROIC (return on invested capital). This assures that all are focused on the same goal.

Jim Ethier
Former CEO and Chairman of Bush Brothers & Co., now Director
Boards of:
- Bush Brothers & Co.
- Kenco
- Clement C. Pappas
- Grocery Manufacturers Association
- National Food Processors Association – Chairman
- American Family Business Foundation
- National Kraut Packers – President
- Beacon Center of Tennessee

Advisory directors receive half the quarterly meeting fee and do not participate in the reward plan.

We would be served as a private company community if some organization would develop a benchmark study of fees for board service.

Note: Jim asked that I not disclose specific numbers, however, I can note that Bush Brothers & Company, although family owned, targets their board compensation to be in the 75th percentile for public companies of comparable size.

Gene Goda

Allow me to offer one specific example of private company board compensation. One individual recently purchased a company under a multi-year buyout agreement. It has established a stock option plan with four-year vesting, providing approximately 30% ownership to key employees

Gene Goda
Consultant, served 22 boards and managed 7 companies in President and CEO positions
Boards of:
▪ Powerwave Technologies
▪ ObjectShare – CEO/Chairman
▪ LightWorks Optics
▪ Nexiant - Chairman

and members of the board. The company has about $15MM in annual revenue, with projected growth potential to $100MM in two years. The board has six in-person meetings per year, and about four telephonic meetings, as needed. Committees have six in-person meetings and are very active. The board consists of one inside owner/director, and seven independent directors.

Board compensation consists of an annual retainer of $12,000, paid monthly in advance, and a per-meeting fee of $1,500, paid at the conclusion of each meeting. Payment also made if attendance by telephone but this is very rare. At present, no additional fees are paid to the lead director, committee chairs, or committee members. This may change in the future when the company achieves certain growth,

EBITDA, and valuation objectives. The stock options granted to independent directors are equivalent to one percent ownership at initial capitalization and are subject to investor dilution, and acceleration of vesting under a change of control. Combined annual cash compensation ranges from $21,000 to $30,000.

This is an established niche company that has a big opportunity on its doorstep. It was clear to the new owner that a good board would be a critical factor in navigating the path ahead. He went about recruiting directors, not based on friendships, but on the strategic expertise needs of the company. In addition to oversight duties, the new board is highly engaged in guiding strategic initiatives that, of course, are intended to create value.

The objective of the owner and management is to achieve an early liquidity event, not to cash-out, but to provide the financial resources to take the company to a higher level. There is good chemistry and energy among the directors – much open discussion and humor to overcome difficult topics. Since everyone is new, we are not bound by old habits or an 'Uncle Fester, or naysayer' lurking in the background. Each director is assigned to help mentor management but acts cautiously to avoid inherent conflicts.

Having served on twenty-four boards (public and private), I feel the compensation plan is right for this unique situation. The focus is on building value for all stakeholders and that means the board has to have a deep commitment and understanding of the risks and strategic initiatives to provide guidance. Everyone's head must be in the game – each providing their unique perspective. While cash comp may be considered low, clearly there is a big payoff if the business achieves its valuation and liquidity objectives. All of the directors are financially independent and are not dependent on the short-term cash. They all demonstrate a quality of commitment and responsiveness that I wish existed in other boards.

My personal belief is simple ... a compensation plan should be molded to fit the needs and objectives of the private/family business. Whatever the plan, the director must be committed to a full measure of service. In this role, the level of compensation must not compromise one's performance of duties.

Don Springer

In service to the shareholders of a private company, board compensation should be structured to create directors' vested interest in the success of the enterprise along side the shareholders whom they serve. This is the case even though there are many motivations for directors joining boards.

To the extent possible then, compensation should be a combination of cash and equity. How much of either is due to many factors: company size, life-cycle stage of the business, type of board (fiduciary or advisory), etc. Startups often can only afford equity while mature companies with no liquidity events on the horizon tend to favor cash over equity.

> **Don Springer**
> Chairman of The Colton Group, Inc.
> Former President of Ford Motor Co. Technology Subsidiary, CEO of Microsoft VAR, CEO of multiple venture- backed startups.
> Boards of:
> - Geometrics Results, Inc., Subsidiary of Ford Motor Co.
> - GRI GmbH, GRI Ltd., & GRI S.A.
> - Knomadix
> - MedSpoke, Inc.
> - Fullscope, Inc.
> - Knowledge Transfer Corporation
> - IMC

Cash compensation is associated with meeting fees, period fees (quarterly or annual), retainers, or some combination thereof. Period fees or retainers tend to provide companies with better access to expertise in these volatile times. They reinforce ad-hoc discussions between formal meetings as the business dynamics change and the needs arise. This is especially the case with startups and distressed companies, but today mature companies are not excluded from frequent disruptions. Even so, some companies prefer to pay meeting fees, whether scheduled or ad-hoc. This usually requires participation in some kind of reward program, equity or other, to bolster on-going director commitment beyond simply meeting preparation.

Compensation should also be the same for all private company board members. This eliminates complexity and pulls the board together to serve as a unit. That said, issue dates and strike price of equity will naturally favor directors who joined a venture earlier.

It all comes back to what the company can afford in attracting the right director expertise and aligning directors' interests with the shareholders.

In Summary

Please keep in mind that the information contained in this chapter is intended to be fairly timeless. While basic governance and board standards and practices tend to be relatively consistent over time, other than periodic corporate regulatory changes, compensation does generally trend up over time. This is due to normal inflationary trends, and to the risks of directorships as perceived by qualified candidates. However, any specific dollar amounts of compensation mentioned above are relevant to a 2016 time period.

In this chapter, I have tried to give my reader a solid basis for understanding and conceptualizing compensation for their board of directors that will yield the maximum return on the significant time and energy necessary to get the full benefit that a well-qualified board can deliver. It is my experience that the largest cost of a board is the time and energy, not the compensation. In that light, I believe that a first-class fiduciary board is one of the best investments any company can make, in terms of the amount of leverage it can provide to your return on investment and enterprise value.

This has been by far the most difficult chapter in this book to write. I truly hope that my readers find it worthwhile.

Additional Background

National Association of Corporate Directors *2014-2015 DIRECTOR COMPENSATION REPORT*

Note: This section contains selected excerpts, data and analysis from the 2014–2015 NACD Private Company Governance Survey, and appears here by permission of the publisher, the National Association of Corporate Directors, (Washington, DC: NACD, 2015). This copyrighted content may not be reproduced or disseminated by any means without prior written consent from NACD. **The information contained in this section represent current thought at the time of publication, however it may be subject to change over time.**

This report provides a comprehensive perspective on director pay practices across a wide range of industries and company sizes - 1,400 companies across twenty-four industries, that filed a proxy statement or other financial statement with director compensation information for the fiscal year ending between Feb. 1, 2013, and Jan. 31, 2014. Companies were assigned to one of twenty-four industries according to their industry classification within Standard & Poor's Global Industry Classification Standard (GICS).

Companies are assigned to one of five size categories on the basis of their annual revenues.

Micro	$50M to $500M	*298 companies*
Small	$500M to $1B	*297 companies*
Medium	$1B to $2.5B	*300 companies*
Large	$2.5B to $10B	*305 companies*
Top 200 companies	*200 largest companies in the S&P 500 on the basis of revenue*	

All companies in this survey are publicly traded.

Principles and Leading Practices for Director Pay

The compensation of non-employee directors is a critical element in the overall governance of any company. Non-employee director compensation has two purposes:

- *To align the interests of shareholders and directors, and*
- *To provide value to directors for value received.*

Five Principles

In meeting these purposes, the following five principles should be used by all companies in setting director compensation.

1. *Director compensation should be determined by the board and disclosed completely to shareholders.*
2. *Director compensation should be aligned with the long-term interest of shareholders.*
3. *Compensation should be used to motivate director behavior.*
4. *Directors should be adequately compensated for their time and effort.*
5. *Director compensation should be approached on an overall basis, rather than as an array of separate elements.*

Leading Practices

Based on these principles, the NACD Blue Ribbon Commission recommends the Leading practices listed below.

A company's board of directors should:

1. *Establish a process by which directors can determine the compensation program in a deliberate and objective way.*
2. *Set a substantial target for stock ownership by each director and a time period during which this target is to be met.*

3. *Define a desirable total value of all forms of director compensation.*

4. *Pay directors solely in the form of equity and cash – with equity representing 50–100% of the total; dismantle the existing benefit programs and avoid creating new ones.*

5. *Adopt a policy stating that a company should not hire a director or a director's firm to provide professional services to the company.*

6. *Disclose fully in the proxy statement the philosophy and process used in determining director compensation and the value of all elements of the compensation program.*

Data Analysis and Methodology

The number of directors on a board increases with company size, ranging from a median of seven directors in the *Micro* category to a median of eleven directors in the Top 200 category.

The issue of diversity in the context of ensuring broad perspective on governance and business strategy continues to be an important one for many boards and is receiving greater attention and scrutiny. Although board diversity can cover many demographics (e.g., ethnicity, gender, experience, etc.), only director gender can be discerned from proxy statement disclosure. The percentage of companies with women board members increases with company size, and this year's study indicates that, although female representation is still well below that of males, notable progress was made across all size categories in terms of female board membership.

Current data also continues the trend away from the combined CEO/chair board leadership structure. With the exception of the *Micro* size category, where the prevalence of combined CEO and board chair remained constant, there was a 3% average decline in the prevalence of a leadership structure in which the CEO and board chair positions were held by the same individual. Overall, the prevalence of a combined role correlates with company size, with 40% to 45% of *Micro* and *Small* companies reporting such a practice, a figure that increases to 63% among *Top 200* companies.

Year-Over-Year Total Direct Compensation Trends

Over the past several years, this report has noted an ongoing trend among boards to eliminate and/or reduce committee pay elements and to instead move that pay into the annual cash retainer or equity grant. Current studies further reinforce that trend, with committee pay declining across all size categories except the *Micro* size category.

Board Pay Elements

Public boards of all sizes rely on a similar mix of cash and equity compensation elements: board cash retainers, board meeting fees, committee pay in the form of retainers and meeting fees, and equity compensation delivered as full-value stock and/or stock options.

The board cash retainer as a portion of TDC generally remains consistent across all size categories, ranging from 31% of TDC at *Medium* companies to 37% at *Micro* companies. Also, with the exception of *Micro* companies, the board cash retainer makes up the second largest portion of total director compensation across all size categories. These percentages remained steady over the prior year, with no size category exhibiting a change of more than 1%. Instead, differentiation in pay practices has generally been driven by the other components of TDC. While equity compensation continues to be the largest component of TDC for all size categories except for *Micro* companies, smaller companies tend to deliver a greater portion of total pay in cash (i.e., cash retainers, board meeting fees, and committee pay) than do the larger companies. Conversely, larger companies deliver the majority of TDC in the form of equity compensation. Board meeting fees and committee pay constitute the smallest portion of TDC, ranging from 1% and 5%, respectively, at the *Top 200* companies to 7% and 11%, respectively, at the *Micro* companies. Lastly, and as we've seen over the past several years, full-value shares continue to be favored over stock options, both in terms of relative value and prevalence.

Board Leadership

Current findings continue to support the trend toward separating the CEO and board chair role. The prevalence of the combined CEO and board chair modestly declined across all size categories, except in the *Micro* size category, where the prevalence remained unchanged. Overall, the prevalence of a combined role correlates with company size, with 40% to 45% of *Micro* and *Small* companies reporting such a practice, and with that figure increasing to 63% of *Top 200* companies.

At companies where the same individual is both board chair and an executive of the company (either as CEO or other executive), many companies appoint an outside director to provide non-executive board leadership. The non-executive board leader generally takes the title of lead independent director or presiding director or some other similar title. This practice has been largely institutionalized by the need to have a non-employee director chair meetings of the independent directors as required by exchange regulations and, by extension, to eliminate the potential of the CEO overseeing his or her own performance.

As companies split the role of CEO and board chair and the prevalence of a combined CEO/board chair decreases, the prevalence of non-executive board chairs has increased. The increase ranges from 1% at *Micro* companies to 5% at *Medium* and *Top 200* companies. Company size generally correlates with board leadership structure with a combined CEO/chair being more prevalent at larger companies.

Premium compensation for non-executive board chairs continues to be well above that for other types of board leadership (e.g., lead director, presiding director, etc.). Premium compensation for non-executive board chairs ranges from 85% in the *Top 200*-size category to 90% in the *Medium* size category. However, the prevalence of premium compensation at companies with other types of board leadership ranges from 61% of companies in the *Micro* size category to 80% in the *Large* size category.

Industry Pay Practices

TDC pay levels vary widely across the twenty-four industries represented in the survey.

Technology and related industries continue to be among the highest-paid boards, as in the past several years. The Pharmaceuticals, Biotechnology, & Life Sciences industry was the highest-paying industry overall and in the *Small*, *Medium*, and *Large* categories. Semiconductors & Semiconductor Equipment led in the *Micro* and *Top 200* categories and was among the three highest-paying industries in four of the five size categories. Rounding out the *Top 200* category were the Technology Hardware & Equipment and Energy industries, respectively.

In line with higher pay for board members, the Pharmaceuticals, Biotechnology, & Life Sciences and Semiconductors & Semiconductor Equipment industries ranked in the top three for highest total board cost across four and three size categories, respectively. In the *Top 200* category, Banks ranked the highest, followed by Technology Hardware & Equipment and Telecommunication Services.

At the bottom end of total board cost, the Transportation industry ranked among the three lowest-paying industries in four of the five size categories. Household & Personal Products; Food, Beverage, & Tobacco; and Food & Staples Retailing industries were among the three lowest-paying industries in two size categories.

Note: please keep in mind that the most of the information contained in this chapter is fairly timeless. However, any specific dollar amounts of compensation are associated with a 2013-2016 time period. Many factors can affect these numbers over time.

Chapter 16

In Conclusion

One of the advantages of writing a book about boards of directors is that it is likely to have a long shelf life. A board's purpose, function, and formal processes, has not changed greatly in about two hundred years. Yet during that same period the global surroundings our boards must navigate have changed dramatically. Everything is much more complex today than in yesteryear, and getting more so. Examples of increasing complexity include national interests, societies, commerce, business, transportation and communication. And, what about monetary systems, business models, government regulations, technology in general, the Internet, security of information, and especially the overall speed of business. Under the circumstances I'd submit that governance models have held up admirably well over the years. However, they are showing strain.

A meeting of a board of directors of the Leipzig-
Dresden Railway Company circ. 1852

Boards of directors certainly existed many years before 1876 when Henry Martyn Robert first published his famous book commonly referred to as *Robert's Rules of Order.* He intended it as a guide for conducting meetings and making decisions as a group. However, the book went on to become the de facto template for 'board meetings' ever since. Both the *Rules* and boards have evolved some over time. However, 'the times they are a-changing', and much faster than any time in the past. The number of critical issues facing boards and management have never been more numerous, more complicated or more threatening. Today's boards must rise to the challenges, or their respective enterprises will become 'road kill.' Sadly, their failures could also be disastrous for shareholders, employees, vendors, customers and yes, communities and countries.

This is the dark side, but there is also a light ahead. Board qualification matrixes, selection methods and basic compensation have shown worthy change over the last decade. Many boards have shown meaningful change for the better, prompted by shareholders, competition, government regulations, and of course just plain good common sense.

The opportunities and rewards for success are larger than ever for those companies that promptly, diligently and thoughtfully address these issues. I also see private companies of all stripes and sizes embracing best-of-class governance practices and boards in greater numbers than at any time in all my five decades as a student of these things. To me, one meaningful example of this trend is the encouragement I have received in writing this book, and of course the fact that you are reading it.

I encourage you to go forth and do your part. Learn all you can about governance and boards, and promote them among the business leaders you share your time with. Seek to form high-performing boards within the enterprises you influence, and aspire to join progressive boards whenever the opportunity presents itself. Share whatever you can with whomever you can. This is your personal fiduciary responsibility to the global community of commerce that spawned us all.

Dennis J. Cagan

Printed in the United States
By Bookmasters